GOOD HEALTH, GOOD TRAVEL

Good Health, Good Travel

A guide for backpackers, travellers, volunteers and overseas workers

Dr Ted Lankester MA, MB, B Chir., MRCGP
Director, InterHealth

with a chapter on Stress by
Dr Ruth Fowke MB, BS, MRCPsych.
Senior Psychiatrist, InterHealth

Hodder & Stoughton
LONDON SYDNEY AUCKLAND
in association with InterHealth, London

First published in Great Britain 1993 by InterHealth in
association with Gospel Communication.
This edition published in Great Britain 1995 by Hodder &
Stoughton.

10 9 8 7 6 5 4 3 2 1

British Library Cataloguing in Publication Data
A record for this book is available from the British Library

ISBN 0 340 64166 5

InterHealth is a registered Christian medical charity which
specialises in the health needs of those serving abroad,
including volunteers, aid workers and mission partners.
InterHealth provides a comprehensive range of health care
support both for individuals and their sending agencies,
irrespective of their religious affiliation. This includes medical
and psychological selection, health examinations on return,
psychiatric support, counselling and debriefing, the provision
of relevant health kits, equipment, medicines and books, and
a comprehensive advisory service.

Typeset by Hewer Text Composition Services, Edinburgh
Printed and bound in Great Britain by
Cox & Wyman Ltd, Reading, Berks.

Hodder and Stoughton Ltd
A division of Hodder Headline PLC
338 Euston Road
London NW1 3BH

This book is dedicated to
my favourite fellow travellers,
Joy, Rachel, Heather and Debbie

CONTENTS

APPENDICES 205

ACKNOWLEDGEMENTS

I would like to thank a number of people for their helpful comments on reading through the draft of this manual. They include the late Dr A. J. Broomhall, Mr Stuart Buchanan of CMS, Dr Denis Roche, previously of Interserve, Dr Mark Evason of Crosslinks, Dr Marianne Janosi, recently retired VSO medical adviser, Dr Mike Jones of Care for Mission, and Mr Steve Price-Thomas, previously of Project Trust, now of VSO. In addition Mr Frank Tovey OBE and Miss Jackie Hall from InterHealth have given invaluable advice.

Responsibility for any errors or shortcomings is entirely my own.

INFORMATION SOURCES

Information in this book is based on authoritative UK and international sources including the World Health Organisation and the UK Malaria Reference Laboratory.

As far as possible information was correct at the time of publication. However, recommendations on travel medicine frequently change, especially with regards to immunisation and antimalarial advice. For this reason the latest edition of this book should always be used or a travel health adviser consulted.

HOW TO USE THIS MANUAL

The purpose of this book is to help you take sensible pre-cautions and then stop worrying about all the things which may, but probably won't, happen to you. Many people over-seas keep in better health than those who remain behind, and the commonest problems are the same conditions, including road accidents, you would encounter at home. You will probably have bouts of diarrhoea and you may get malaria, but gruesome tropical conditions are thankfully rare.

Parts of the manual are designed for reading through, others are designed for reference.

Here is a suggested plan of action:

READING THROUGH:

Before you go read through the whole of Section 1 and relevant parts of Section 2. Also glance through the Appendices.

When overseas read relevant parts of Section 2.

Before coming home or on arrival in the UK read Section 3.

REFERENCE:

Section 4, Notes on Important Conditions, is largely for you to refer to abroad when you become concerned or affected by particular conditions.

EVALUATION:

Please let us know what you think of this book. We are continually wanting to update and improve our information and health briefing. When you get back home, take a few minutes to complete the evaluation page and send it to us at InterHealth.

SECTION 1

BEFORE YOU GO

CHECK LIST BEFORE YOU LEAVE

There is a great deal to do just before leaving and it's all too easy if you are normally healthy, or very laid back, to leave health matters to the last moment. By planning well ahead, especially for immunisations, you actually save yourself time – and a lot of last-minute hassle.

For all except the shortest journeys to the healthiest places you will need to do the following:

● Complete all necessary *immunisations* (see pages 4–10).

● Obtain any *certificates* that may be required, e.g. yellow fever and occasionally cholera and freedom from HIV (see pages 228, 218 and 84 respectively).

● Take sufficient *antimalarials* (see pages 14, 66–71).

● Take a pack of *sterile needles* and *syringes* (see page 11 and Appendix B).

● Consider taking an appropriate *first aid/medical/AIDS protection/dental kit* (see pages 10–14 and Appendices A, B and C).

● Take other *personal supplies*, including medicines, contraceptives etc (see pages 12–16).

● Know your *blood group*, and keep a written record with you (see pages 88–9).

● Discover any particular *health or security hazards* of the country you are visiting or special precautions that are recommended.

● Visit a *dentist* and have all dental work completed.

● Visit an *optician* for a routine eye check, if going on a long journey (see page 151).

● Plan ahead for *self-entertainment* and *professional update* if going to a remote area or prolonged assignment (see pages 18–20, 114–17).

● Find out about any *reciprocal health arrangements* in the country you are going to (see pages 26–7).

● If going to an EU country complete *form E111* and have it stamped.

● Consider having a *medical examination*, especially if you have any known health problems, are over the age of 50 or are going to a developing country for longer than six months (see pages 16–18).

● Take out *health insurance* unless arranged by your company or agency (see pages 26–7).

● Women should be up-to-date with their *cervical smear tests*.

● Consider going on a *first aid course*, especially if going to a remote area or leading a team or expedition.

● Check all *travel documents* and work out a *safe system* for keeping money and travel documents (see pages 120–2).

● Make a *will*.

● *Photocopy important documents* including main page of your passport and any outward or return air tickets and keep photocopies separately, along with numbers of travellers' cheques.

● Make it up with your *mother-in-law* (or anyone else) as unresolved conflicts can add to overseas stress.

● Be *well-prepared medically* but don't allow worries about health to overshadow or dominate your time abroad.

ARRANGING YOUR IMMUNISATIONS

A journey to a clinic or surgery with a resultant sore muscle is a small price to pay for protection from several nasty diseases. It is, however, worth noting that less that one disease episode in ten when overseas is preventable by a vaccine. This means that following antimalarial precautions, advice on food and water, and accident prevention is even more important than being jabbed at your local health centre.

The menu of immunisations available is lengthening all the time. Some are *essential* for everyone but others depend on weighing up risk and benefit. This means your health adviser will need to know the *area* you will be living in, the *occupation* you will be engaged in, and the *length of time* you will be staying, in order to give you appropriate advice (see below). Even then different doctors or advisers may give you different advice (see page 8).

HOW SHOULD I SET ABOUT HAVING IMMUNISATIONS?

Here are some guidelines:

1. Discover which immunisations you will need

If you are travelling independently ask your GP or practice nurse for advice, or visit a travel clinic (see Appendix D, pages 211–15).

If going with a company or sending agency, you will normally be provided with a list of recommended immunisations for your trip. If you are not, ask for one.

2. Work out a time schedule

Do this with the doctor or nurse likely to be giving these to you (usually your own GP surgery). If you have been given a list of recommended immunisations take this with you. Let the clinic work out a schedule with you, rather than spend too much time working out your own scheme. Usually immunisations can be completed in two or three visits to the surgery or travel clinic.

3. Allow plenty of time to fit them all in

If going to a developing country try to allow three months unless you have travelled in the past three years. This way you will be able to complete courses without having to take vaccine with you. If you don't have this much time, your schedule can usually be telescoped.

4. Understand the spacing rules

If you are one of those travellers who like to keep track of what is being done to you, read on!

● You can have two or more non-live vaccines together.

● You can have one live and one or more non-live vaccines together.

● You can have two live vaccines together, but if they are not given on the same day they should be at least three weeks apart (because of effectiveness, not safety).

● If using gammaglobulin you should ideally have this at least three weeks after (or three months before) any live vaccine except yellow fever. This is again because of effectiveness, not safety. If you are in a hurry this rule can be set aside, with minimal effect.

● Leave gammaglobulin to the week before you go because as with cholera it loses its effectiveness quicker than others.

Note: (1) for trips over three months hepatitis A vaccine is generally preferred to gammaglobulin; (2) live vaccines are oral polio, BCG, yellow fever, mumps, measles, rubella, oral typhoid, and live oral cholera. All the rest are non-live.

WHAT IMMUNISATIONS ARE NEEDED?

A. Immunisations recommended for *all* developing countries, for which you must be in-date before leaving:

Adults

Hepatitis A (or gammaglobulin)
Polio
Tetanus
Typhoid

Children

BCG (for TB)
DPT (diphtheria, pertussis, tetanus)

Hepatitis A (not usually under age 10)
Hib (Haemophilus influenzae b)
Polio
MMR (mumps, measles, rubella)
Typhoid (not under eighteen months)

B. Immunisations needed for *some* developing countries depending on your location, occupation and length of time abroad:

Cholera (usually for the sake of the certificate)
Diphtheria for adults (usually combined with tetanus)
Hepatitis B
Japanese encephalitis
Meningitis
Rabies
Yellow fever (you must also obtain a certificate)

C. Immunisations only rarely needed:

Influenza
Measles for adults
Mumps
Plague
Rubella (for women of child-bearing age with no immunity)
Tick-borne encephalitis

In addition Anti D Immunoglobulin may be needed by some Rhesus negative women who become pregnant or plan an overseas delivery (see page 128).

TAKING BOOSTER DOSES WITH YOU

Sometimes it is not possible to complete a course of immunisations before you leave.

Although most vaccines will keep for a short time unrefrigerated it is better to carry them in a chilled vacuum flask containing a sealed ice pack and then put them into a fridge on arrival. *Vaccines should not be frozen and therefore should not be put in the aircraft hold.* Yellow fever should not be taken with you.

Some GPs or travel clinics will provide supplies for overseas. When abroad they should be given by a doctor or nurse using a sterile syringe and needle. They must be kept reliably cold between 2° and 8°C unless otherwise specified.

WHERE TO HAVE IMMUNISATIONS DONE

Although travel clinics can give all immunisations, you can save yourself money by having NHS eligible jabs performed by your GP surgery. The following are normally available on the NHS (Group 1):

Cholera
Hepatitis A (or gammaglobulin)
Hepatitis B for doctors, nurses and health workers
Polio
Tetanus
Typhoid
Plus DPT, polio, Hib, MMR and rubella for children.

Occasionally you will have to pay a prescription charge, and a fee for a cholera certificate.

The following are not normally available on the NHS (Group 2):

BCG
Hepatitis B (for non-health workers)
Japanese encephalitis
Meningitis
Rabies
Yellow fever (which is only available from specially licensed surgeries and travel clinics)

Some doctors may be willing to reduce or waive fees for certain immunisations in Group 2 if you are going to be involved in charitable work. Do remember that this is at the doctor's or nurse's discretion and that you have no right to demand free travel jabs.

DIFFERING ADVICE!

It can be bewildering (and annoying) when different doctors seem to give different advice. It helps to understand some of the reasons: correct advice changes frequently both because of new vaccines and differing country-by-country recommendations: experts do not always agree. Advice from UK sources is not always the same as that of our European or North American colleagues. For many immunisations risk and benefit have to be weighed against each other.

It is usually simplest to follow the advice of one person. If going with a company or agency follow their medical adviser's recommendations; otherwise follow advice from your GP or practice nurse.

PREGNANCY AND BREASTFEEDING

Live vaccines (see list on page 6) and cholera should be avoided *in pregnancy*. Non-live vaccines should only be given if going to very high-risk areas, except for gammaglobulin and tetanus which are safe.

All vaccinations can be given *when breastfeeding*.

SPECIAL NOTE FOR PARENTS OF CHILDREN

Children going abroad need even more jabs than their friends staying in the UK. By following a few simple rules, the trauma for them (and for you) can be reduced:

• Be laid back when going to the doctor.

• Tell them, preferably on the way to the clinic and almost in passing, that they will be having a jab. Mention it may hurt a little, but not very much.

• Don't build up to the event, and don't pile on sympathy.

• Have a sweet or treat ready to encourage the last-minute falterer or to use as a bribe or reward.

• Follow the doctor's or nurse's instruction, and hold firmly.

• Try not to let your child see the nurse preparing the injection.

• Use paracetamol suspension (Calpol) over the next few hours and during the first night if the child seems fretful.

SPECIAL NOTE FOR EXPERIENCED TRAVELLERS

As a seasoned traveller or long-term expatriate you may assume that your hard-won immunity removes the need for immunisations. Your risks are not much less than for the first-time traveller. Follow standard immunisation advice like everyone else.

NOTES ON INDIVIDUAL VACCINES

Appendix F gives fuller details on the main vaccines mentioned above.

HEALTH KITS, MEDICINES AND SUPPLIES

What you choose to take with you will obviously depend on many factors – your location, basic health, occupation, leisure pursuits, amount of travel off the beaten path, length of proposed stay, and probably above all your personality.

Here are some medical items to consider for your stay in a

developing country. *Recommended contents of different kits along with lists of suppliers are given in Appendix B.* Contents of kits can be combined, but because travellers' requirements differ so much from one place to another, it is helpful to consider their contents separately.

NEEDLES AND SYRINGES

In many developing countries needles and syringes are reused without adequate cleaning. Even in hospitals and clinics with generally good reputations it is hard to know if the nurse drawing up your injection in the next room is using a sterile needle or not.

Those parts of the world where needles and syringes are in shortest supply often coincide with areas where HIV infection is most common. Quite apart from a small HIV risk, contaminated needles can also give you abscesses, hepatitis B and other viral infections.

Having packed a needle and syringe kit you must remember to have it with you when you need it. Rather more difficult is to insist that the doctor or nurse uses it. This may require courage and tact but if you fail to ask, you may worry about it afterwards.

Customs officials rarely seem to object when they come across medical supplies in your personal luggage. However you should always have a signed doctor's note with you – preferably in your travel documents – which states that these supplies are for your personal, medical use only. Those travelling to a few countries, e.g. Malaysia, Singapore, should avoid taking needles and syringes because of the risk of being misidentified as a drug addict.

AIDS PROTECTION KIT

Blood transfusions are a serious HIV and hepatitis B risk in a growing number of countries. In the poorest countries of Africa, south Asia and Latin America, blood is often obtained through private suppliers who may buy blood from those living on the streets, many of whom will be HIV positive. Screening is often inadequate, or non-existent.

You should therefore avoid a 'blind' blood transfusion in a developing country except in a life-threatening emergency. The purpose of the AIDS protection kit is to enable two or more bottles of plasma substitute to be given to you, either to avoid the need for blood altogether, or to tide you over until blood can be given from a trusted donor (see pages 86–9).

The AIDS kit consists of an intravenous giving set and plasma substitute, going under various trade names such as Gelofusine. It can only be used by someone familiar with putting up an intravenous line, such as a medical travelling companion or a trained onlooker at any accident. This does mean there is a possibility the kit cannot be used at the time you need it. Many experts still consider it is better to have one with you in case it can be used, than not to have one at all. The worst scenario is to be in an accident, need your kit, have a trained nurse on site but to have left your kit in the cupboard at home, but also remember not to let it overheat in a hot car boot.

Consider taking an AIDS kit if you are planning to travel widely in any country of sub-Saharan Africa, Latin America (particularly Brazil), the Indian subcontinent and SE Asia (particularly Thailand). They should be taken with you on road journeys or when flying in light aircraft. Any colleague travelling with you should know that you have one, and should also know your blood group (see page 88).

FIRST AID KIT

All travellers need basic first aid equipment, including plasters, scissors, bandages etc. The longer-term resident or intrepid traveller will need more comprehensive supplies (see pages 205–9).

MEDICAL KIT AND PERSONAL MEDICINES

This should contain a basic supply of both over-the-counter and prescription medicines you may need when abroad.

Although many countries sell a range of medicines, supplies may be unreliable and in some countries markets are flooded with fake medicines.

A medical kit is of most value if it is difficult to reach a good hospital known to have a reliable supply of essential medicines. It is also worth having one if you plan to travel in remote areas, on holiday, after an assignment, or during a 'gap' year.

Carry a doctor's letter and list of contents in your hand luggage in case either foreign customs or, on return, British customs, raise any questions.

Make sure you also take with you ample supplies of any permanent medication you may be taking. GPs *may* be willing to prescribe enough for a few weeks on the NHS, but after that you will need to ask your GP or another doctor for a private prescription. If you are going abroad for more than a year consider having further supplies sent out or, better still, brought out to you.

Remember that all medicines have both a trade name (usually in bold print), which varies from place to place, and a generic name (usually in small print) which is the worldwide scientific name. You should get used to recognising and using the generic name. In this manual generics are first, with common trade names afterwards in brackets.

Where possible it is better to take medicines as blister packs or in bottles well packed with cotton wool to prevent transit damage, especially when backpacking. Make sure the tops of ointment tubes are firmly done up, especially at high altitude. Having arrived at your destination keep your supplies in a cool place, out of direct sunlight and away from the reach of rats, ants – and children.

If you use *contact lenses* take plenty of cleansing fluid as well as a pair of glasses. If you are a *diabetic* take all supplies you may need with you (but see page 139).

Women should take a supply of *sanitary towels* unless your enquiries confirm that reliable and acceptable supplies are available where you are going.

A note on expiry dates. Many medicines have a use-by

date two to four years from the date of manufacture. This means some items in your medical kit are likely to pass their expiry date if your assignment is long-term. However, many medicines if well stored and neither crumbling, damp nor discoloured, will remain both safe and effective for some time after their expiry date, though this cannot be guaranteed.

DENTAL KIT

Emergency dental kits are worth taking if you are travelling for any length of time in remote areas where dentists are few and far between, or where there is a high level of HIV infection (see page 202).

ANTIMALARIALS (See also pp. 58ff)

If you are travelling to a malarious part of the world *it is essential to take antimalarials*. Usually it is easier and cheaper to take these from the UK, rather than buy them abroad, unless you have personal knowledge of a reliable overseas supply. You should include *both* malaria prophylactics (pills to prevent malaria) *and*, if living or travelling in areas remote from good medical care, an emergency supply of standby tablets for treatment. See pages 67–70 for the names of tablets recommended for different areas.

Some antimalarials (e.g. chloroquine and proguanil (Paludrine)) are available from chemists without a prescription. All others have to be prescribed by your GP (there is usually a charge) or obtained from travel clinics. See Appendix D, page 211.

If you are going to an area where malaria is common, or where chloroquine-resistant malaria is known to occur, you may still get malaria even if you take your tablets regularly. You should therefore consider taking these further supplies with you:

● A *mosquito net*, preferably pre-soaked in the safe mosquito-killer, permethrin. Try to find out if a net is available at your destination. Take extra permethrin to resoak your net if you are going for longer than six months.

● *Insect repellent*: take plenty of this, ideally a brand containing DEET (see page 63).

• *Coils* or, better, *vapourising mats* help keep mosquitoes at bay (see page 65).

ORAL CONTRACEPTIVES

Because supplies usually have to be taken with you it is worth planning what contraception to use well before leaving. If you are using the pill for the first time try to take two or three cycles before you go abroad to make sure it suits you.

Suggestions for those taking the pill when travelling

• *Ample supplies*. Take plenty with you unless you know the pill of your choice is available overseas. There are many brand names for each pill, so keep a packet cover with you which will have both the brand name and exact formulation written on it. Split your supply between different parts of your baggage in case of theft.

Your GP may be willing to prescribe enough for up to three months, your family planning clinic possibly for longer. Otherwise you can obtain a private prescription from your GP, or from some travel clinics. Make sure all your supplies expire after the latest date you might need them.

• *Time zones*. When crossing these make sure you take a pill at least every twenty-four hours, preferably at the same time, until you gradually adjust to your new timetable. During this adjustment the time between pills can be less than twenty-four hours but should not be longer.

• *Diarrhoea*, stomach upsets and courses of antibiotics (in particular ampicillin and tetracycline) can reduce absorption of the pill. In such situations take the pill as usual, avoid having sex or use an additional method of contraception during these risk periods and for seven days after. If these seven days coincide with your gap of seven pill-free days, ignore this gap and start straight in with the next cycle of pills.

• *Vomiting*. If this occurs within three hours of taking a pill, take another. If vomiting then continues, use additional protection as above.

• *Avoiding periods* when travelling. You can do this for one or two cycles by taking the pill continuously. If you plan to do this, take extra packs with you. It may be possible for you to use this method even if you do not take the pill for contraception – discuss this with your doctor well before leaving.

● *Types of pill*. A fixed combination oestrogen-progestogen pill is probably the most appropriate. This is usually known as the combined contraceptive pill. The progestogen-only pill is less appropriate for travel and gives less good protection, especially when crossing time zones, or with stomach upsets. Biphasic and triphasic pills with dose formulations which vary with the time of the month, are less flexible for travelling.

● *Hepatitis*. If you go down with this it is best to avoid the pill for six months.

● *Hot climates*. Pills should remain effective provided your pack is within the expiry date, it remains intact and you keep it in as cool a place as possible.

● *Condoms*. If you think you may need these take a supply with you, rather than depend on those made locally.

WATER STERILISATION

There are two situations where *water filters* are useful:

● *On the road* when you need a light, quick, portable method of purifying water.

● *If setting up home* where boiling is not an easy option (e.g. in a fuel-deficient area), take with you or buy locally a filter system suitable for producing larger supplies of clean water. When travelling, always have with you a supply of *water-sterilising tablets* (see page 42 and Appendix C for suppliers).

MEDICAL EXAMINATION BEFORE GOING ABROAD

If you are travelling independently consider having a medical examination if you plan to be abroad for six months or more, if you are over 50, or if you are planning any especially arduous pursuits such as mountaineering or scuba diving. If you have any serious or recurrent health problems you should talk to your doctor before going on any trip outside western Europe.

If you are going overseas on an assignment for more than three to six months, your organisation will probably ask you to have a medical. For shorter trips you may be asked to fill in a medical form and to request your GP also to complete one from your medical records. Although the point of these is largely to see whether you are fit or not, they also help in the choice of an appropriate location and assignment if you do have any pre-existing health problems (see pages 20–6).

You may be going with one of the increasing number of organisations who are asking applicants to be seen by a psychiatrist or clinical psychologist. Sometimes psychometric testing is also included. Don't be taken aback by this. The main purpose is not to exclude people from going abroad but to help ensure that your own placement is consistent with your gifts and temperament.

When you do have a medical or have to complete a question-naire it is worth being complete (and honest). Holding back information isn't doing yourself a favour. Questions asked are mainly to protect your health in situations where health care may be poor quality, and to make sure you are placed in a safe and appropriate location.

Medicals are often carried out by the medical officer of the organisation you will be working with. An increasing number are done by doctors who specialise in travel medicine.

GPs also carry out pre-travel medical examinations, but you are not entitled to this on the NHS. The GP's charge is at their own discretion but they are entitled to ask up to £51.50 for a full medical. If you are going abroad as a volunteer, aid worker or mission partner, some GPs are prepared to reduce their fees, but this is entirely at their discretion.

If you do not know your blood group, or that of other family members, this is a good time to find out. Your GP may be willing to arrange this but there is usually a charge. Alternatively you can give blood, though it may occasionally take several weeks before your donor card with a note of your blood group is sent to you.

Certain conditions preclude you from giving blood in the UK, including: hepatitis within the past year, being a hepatitis B or C carrier, pregnancy, any skin piercing within the past year, any past homosexual encounter, history of self-injections with drugs, high blood pressure or diabetes/epilepsy requiring medication.

Phone the National Blood Transfusion Service on 0345-711711 for further details of how and where to give blood.

PREPARING FOR AN OVERSEAS ASSIGNMENT

If you are planning to spend any length of time in a new country, it is worth learning as much as possible about its customs and lifestyle. Apart from being interesting in itself this has two main benefits: it helps to reduce your own culture shock on arrival, and it also makes it less likely that you will cause offence to the local people by dressing or behaving in a way that is out of keeping with local traditions. This can be especially important in Muslim countries.

Here are a few suggestions:

● *Meeting people*. There may be people from the country you will be visiting who are studying or living in the UK. It can be mutually enriching getting to know them and discovering something of their beliefs and lifestyle.

It is also valuable talking to any expatriate who has actually lived in or visited the area you are going to. By asking specific questions you will be able to prepare yourself both mentally and practically. It will give you a chance to find out what items are locally available and what clothes and personal belongings you should take with you.

● *Reading*. Time allowing, it is worth reading history books, travel books, novels, and any literature covering your own profession or field of interest. Selective reading of a travel guide, e.g the 'Rough Guides' or the 'Lonely Planet' series, helps to give ideas for leisure activities.

● *Watching films*, videos, TV programmes or cultural events (art exhibits, dances, drama) of the country you are visiting.

The wider your background knowledge the greater will be your appreciation and understanding of what you see – and the more appropriate your contribution while overseas.

● *Learning some language*. A little can go a long way, stimulate interest and help to give you a head start when you wander through the bazaar or join the language school.

You will probably be able to find someone here who speaks the language you need to learn. Alternatively select the most appropriate language guide or consider using a Linguaphone or BBC course.

● *Adjusting expectations* to a sensible level, especially in terms of your job or assignment. This is especially important for goal-orientated professionals who will need to learn that people are often more important than projects, good local relationships of greater value than a list of achievements in newsletters home.

In terms of time management, it helps to realise before you go that the process of living, e.g. shopping, cooking, communicating, travelling, may often take many times longer than at home, effectively reducing your 'productive' working life by half. You may need to spend a day each year, or even a day each month, sitting in an office to obtain a permit, visa, or permission for something absurdly trivial. Being prepared for delays, inefficiency, corruption and red tape enables you to use productively time spent waiting (e.g. language-swotting, knitting, reading) rather than prolonging the process by outbursts of expatriate anger.

● *Discovering ways* to minimise cultural differences. Clothes and gadgets should be selected and worn with care. The uncovered arms or legs of women may be quite acceptable in some countries, but enough to cause stones to fly in others. Photographic and electronic wizardry may draw gasps of admiration from the local inhabitants, but at the expense of you being seen as a provider of foreign merchandise rather than as a straightforward friend.

● *Avoiding gaffes*. Customs, habits and clothes which we take for granted may cause offence or amusement in other cultures. Do some homework first so as to avoid gaffes which can put your local acceptance rating back to zero. Classic examples include eating or giving gifts with the left hand, baring your flesh in public (e.g. Muslim countries), and failing to remove your shoes when entering a local home. Passing wind may cause amusement – or extreme offence – travellers with Giardia please note.

● *Preparing for leisure*. Before going abroad decide to build into your lifestyle adequate leisure and time off. In practice this can be difficult if you live in a remote area, travel is dangerous, or you are confined within the four walls of a hospital, training centre or compound. A few well-chosen books, games, raw materials for a creative hobby (e.g. oil paints) and a pair of binoculars can pay off huge dividends.

● *Decide to keep a diary or record*. Quite apart from being fun to read to yourself in twelve months' time, or to grandchildren in future years, it helps you to see your life in perspective. Sometimes writing down a difficult, annoying or frightening episode can deprive it of its sting. It also stimulates you to continue being a student of the country in which you are living.

● *Orientation course*. Most sending agencies or large companies run training courses, briefing weekends or even residential terms for preparation. If one hasn't been arranged try to join one. By helping you to think through situations before they occur, you will be better able to handle the human, emotional, physical and spiritual conditions you are likely to meet.

● Finally consider doing a Teaching English as a Foreign Language (TEFL) or Teaching English as a Second Language (TESL) course, a week on vehicle maintenance, and, especially if you are going as a team leader, a first aid course run by the local branch of the British Red Cross or St John/ St Andrew's Ambulance.

PRECAUTIONS FOR TRAVELLERS WITH SPECIAL CONDITIONS

If you suffer from any serious or long-standing illness or disability it is worth having a medical examination before finalising any overseas travel, and discussing dangers, precautions and medication in detail with your doctor. The points made here do not replace the personal advice your own doctor will give you.

If you are under a specialist you should discuss with him the pros and cons of your proposed journey and ask for any tips about how to minimise your health risks.

Some medical conditions will debar you from international flights:

- Pregnancy at thirty-five weeks or beyond.
- Abdominal surgery within the past ten days, chest surgery within fourteen days.
- Recent stroke, heart attack, heart failure, severe angina.
- Any chest condition causing breathlessness at rest.
- Any acute infectious illness.
- Severe anaemia.
- Severe mental disturbance without escort and sedation.
- Severe ear and sinus infections. Recent ear surgery.
- Bleeding from a peptic ulcer within the past three weeks.
- Uncontrolled or unstable epilepsy.
- Plaster casts (trapped air may expand – consider splitting).

HEART PROBLEMS

It is generally unwise to visit a developing country or to take up residence abroad within three to six months of having a confirmed *heart attack*.

If you have suffered from *any serious heart disease* or remain under treatment make sure that your future location and occupation are unlikely to cause undue strain. Try to organise your actual travel to be as stress-free as possible. Have someone with you who can carry your luggage, or arrange in advance with the airline to use a wheelchair.

Precautions overseas include: living within reasonable access of adequate health care, and avoiding unduly stressful, hot or humid conditions. An air conditioner is a good investment. It is hard to generalise about altitude as ability to tolerate this is so variable. Discuss any exposure to altitudes over 2,000 metres (about 6,500 feet) with your doctor.

Some *blood pressure tablets* may lead to increased giddiness in hot climates and in addition tablets called betablockers can cause shortness of breath at higher altitudes. If your blood pressure has been raised in the past have this checked at least once every three months or as your doctor advises.

Carry copies of ECGs (EKGs) with you, especially your most recent and that taken at the time of any heart attack. This can be most valuable should you have any chest pain and need a further ECG whilst overseas.

Travellers taking *anticoagulants* must ensure that facilities for checking prothrombin time or an equivalent are present at the point of destination and that adequate doses are taken to cover flights when the risk of leg thrombosis increases. Make sure that no travel medication you are given affects the dose.

Those with *pacemakers* should tell security officials. Although devices in international airports in western countries are set so as not to cause problems, this is not always the case in developing countries.

RESPIRATORY PROBLEMS

Asthma is unpredictable abroad, many travellers improving, some suffering more severe problems. The pollution of many tropical cities, e.g. Cairo, Karachi, Mexico City, Delhi, Calcutta and Kathmandu may cause it to worsen.

Because asthma is so unpredictable and the range of overseas situations so large, it is worth getting specific first-hand information from someone who has been living in the area you are planning to visit. If your asthma is severe, it may be worth making a short trial visit to test out a location for yourself.

Take a supply of the medication you would need for the *worst* attack you have recently suffered. This will probably include an inhaler (e.g. Ventolin and/or Becotide), and may include steroid tablets and antibiotics. Dry powder systems such as Rotahaler and Spinhaler can get clogged in humid climates, and sealed dry powder systems such as Turbohaler and Diskhaler are probably better. A few people may want to take a nebuliser (requires reliable electricity, compatible plugs, battery drive etc) but an excellent alternative is the Nebuhaler, with face mask for children, used for example with the drug terbutaline (Bricanyl).

Work out an action plan with your normal medical adviser so that you know exactly how to use the medicines you take with you, and when you should seek medical advice. If you are a more severe asthmatic it is worth taking a peakflow meter with you and keeping an accurate record of your readings.

Sinusitis is also unpredictable, usually becoming worse in dusty or polluted areas, though often improving elsewhere (until you return to Britain in winter).

Coughs and colds usually continue as usual, especially in families. Hay fever commonly improves.

STOMACH DISORDERS

Peptic ulcers commonly recur overseas especially under stress but are easily treated with modern drugs. A history of past or present *ulcerative colitis* will need very careful assessment and may worsen when overseas, especially after attacks of diarrhoea. *Crohn's disease* also needs caution. If you have these conditions consult a specialist or GP familiar with travel medicine. *Irritable bowel syndrome* may worsen, e.g. after repeated bouts of diarrhoea, but would not normally stop you from travelling. Those with well-controlled *coeliac disease* usually survive travel quite well providing they do research on the local food and availability of gluten-free products before travelling and take extra care to avoid diarrhoea.

A history of *bleeding from the rectum*, usually put down to piles, should be carefully checked by a doctor before you go overseas. Any hernia should be repaired before leaving.

HEADACHES

Both *migraine* and *tension headache* often become worse overseas especially when under stress, or when dehydrated. If you have significant headaches it is worth consulting your doctor to discuss how best you can manage these. Take with you a supply of your favourite painkillers and work out an appropriate lifestyle (see also pages 90–6).

SKIN CONDITIONS

Psoriasis improves in the sun but can worsen under stress. Chloroquine can also make it worse. *Eczema* may flare up in hot or humid climates or with swimming and is more likely to become infected. Widespread, infected eczema is a dangerous condition in the tropics. Ensure your eczema is well controlled before travelling and take a copious supply of all the creams you are likely to need, plus a broad-spectrum antibiotic. *Fungal infections*, especially of the toes (athlete's foot) and of the groin commonly get worse. Take appropriate cream or powder with you (see also pages 194–7).

KIDNEY AND BLADDER PROBLEMS

Kidney stones are common in those who live in the tropics. If you have previously suffered the agony of passing one, ask your GP if an abdominal X-ray and ultrasound can be arranged before you go, to make sure no others are lurking. Keep your fluid intake up, by drinking far more than usual, ideally enough to keep your urine pale. *Bladder infections (cystitis)*, especially in women, can be brought on by long or bumpy car journeys, especially in the heat; or by sexual activity. Treat these with antibiotics, and plenty of fluids (see page 203). Men who have symptoms of *prostate trouble* should have this checked by a doctor before any long-term assignment overseas.

PREVIOUS SPLENECTOMY

If you have previously had your spleen removed you are at slightly greater risk of picking up infections while travelling. It is very important to have a meningitis vaccine if travelling anywhere outside the UK. Also take extra care to avoid getting malaria.

Some aid agencies are reluctant to accept those who have had a splenectomy for any long-term or remote assignment.

BACK AND JOINT PROBLEMS

Minor *aches and pains* often improve in warm climates; *arthritis* is unpredictable. *Backache* can be worsened or caused by the rigours of travel. If you have had recent severe backache or sciatica make sure you seek medical advice before you travel (see page 161).

OVERWEIGHT

Being markedly overweight makes overseas travel more difficult. In a hot climate, tiredness, difficulty in keeping up with others, slowness in acclimatising and a greater tendency to skin infections can all take their toll. Start losing weight before you go rather than assuming it will happen automatically as you head off for the tropics. Many people actually put on weight overseas.

PSYCHOLOGICAL PROBLEMS

As a general rule those embarking on an overseas assignment or adventure travel should be mentally healthy. The stresses and strains of working in a developing country are considerable and psychological problems are one of the commonest causes for emergency repatriation or for cutting short an assignment.

If you feel worried about going abroad because of previous emotional problems or mental illness, see your doctor. Some organisations sending people to frontline or long-term placements will ask applicants to see a psychiatrist or a clinical psychologist before they are accepted.

Depression often (but by no means always) recurs under prolonged, difficult conditions. If you are prone to *anxiety*, counselling or advice on stress management can be helpful. Those who have had *psychotic* illnesses or a recent history of *alcohol abuse*, should generally avoid overseas assignments. If you *smoke*, try hard to give it up before travelling; it increases your risk of becoming ill. Volunteers who have suffered from *anorexia* or *bulimia* in the past (or present) are encouraged to discuss this openly with their sending agency and at any medical.

DIABETES

See pages 138–9.

HEALTH INSURANCE FOR TRAVEL ABROAD

If you are travelling *independently* it is essential to take out an insurance policy which covers the cost of treatment overseas, emergency repatriation and the cost of any delays if accident or illness cause an extended stay. This is usually part of an overall travel insurance policy, which also includes life assurance and insurance of baggage. If you are planning any adventure sports including mountaineering, scuba diving, water or winter sports, make sure your policy includes any resultant accident; and read the small print.

Remember that those over a certain age, usually 65, or who have any serious pre-existing illness, will need to pay an extra premium.

If you are working overseas *with a sending agency or company*, health insurance will probably be arranged for you, but make sure. This will either be through a regular insurance scheme, or through the organisation itself guaranteeing to pay all or a proportion of necessary treatment abroad, or repatriation in an emergency. Ask your organisation about its policy and consider taking out additional insurance if it doesn't meet your requirements. For any visit to the USA you must have full health insurance (up to £5 million) to cover against potentially enormous medical fees.

It is not possible at the present time to take out insurance against the risk of contracting HIV infection, even from an occupational source.

Make yourself aware of any 'reciprocal health care' you may be entitled to in your host country.

Within the European Union, and in some other countries, reciprocal health arrangements are available for British citizens. In order to make use of this you will need to produce your passport, NHS medical card and form E111. The latter is found in the booklet, *Health Advice for Travellers*, available from any post office. The E111 has to be completed and stamped before it is valid (at a post office for a holiday in Europe, at the DSS Newcastle Office if going to live in Europe – see details on form E111). Health cover in Europe is less comprehensive than under the NHS in the UK, and some items will be excluded. Keep all receipts and proofs of purchase of medicines or treatment.

Outside the European Union, some countries offer certain free or subsidised health facilities. Further details can be found in *Health Advice for Travellers*. In practice there are virtually no reciprocal arrangements with most developing countries. When travelling make sure you have a readily available means of paying for any hospital bills.

SPECIAL SCHEMES FOR CHARITABLE WORKERS

Some insurance companies are now providing special insurance packages for those working with charitable organisations. One scheme which is both comprehensive and economic is run by Banner Financial Services in co-operation with International SOS Assistance and the Blood Care Foundation. See Appendix D for details.

PREPARATION FOR THE FLIGHT

Flying is extremely safe, and for many people enjoyable. Usually any pre-flight nerves quickly settle as the plane takes off, and thoughts of distant places (or an impending hot bath at home) take over.

COMMON PROBLEMS OF FLYING AND WAYS OF DEALING WITH THEM

Travel sickness

For children the drive to the airport is as likely to cause nausea as the flight itself. Give your favourite sickness pill in plenty of time, and take spares for any subsequent journeys overseas and the return flight. Hyoscine (Kwells) is a favourite brand, especially for children, and promethazine (Avomine), dimenhydrinate (Dramamine), Boots Travel Sickness Pills and cinnarizine (Stugeron) – not for children under 5 – each have their followers. They are available over the counter.

Remember to take sickness pills at least two hours before their effects are needed, though one hour is sufficient for Kwells, twenty to thirty minutes for Boots. All, except Stugeron, cause a degree of drowsiness, often manifested in children by either greater or lesser charm than usual at check-in.

Cabin pressure

For most planes this is maintained at the pressure normally found at an altitude of 6,000 to 7,000 feet above sea level. This explains why body gases expand, especially in stomachs and ears, and why the amount of oxygen slightly decreases, the latter important only to those with severe heart or lung problems.

You can ease distension of the stomach by wearing loose clothing, avoiding excessive carbonated drinks, eating slowly and avoiding large meals. Ear problems can usually be prevented by sucking a sweet during take-off and landing, or by regular jaw-opening or swallowing. Those with sensitive ears, including children with recent ear infections or catarrh, should have Actifed either by tablet or syrup at the recommended dose for age, one hour before take-off and again before landing. This too is available over the counter.

In-flight drinks and food

Cabin air is extremely dry and dehydration occurs on all long flights. Alcohol, tea and coffee unfortunately make dehydration worse (they cause you to lose more urine than the fluid you take in) and you are best to stick to frequent soft, uncarbonated drinks and fruit juices.

It is a cause of regret to many, not least the returning aid worker and volunteer, that alcohol, fizzy drinks and large, rich meals are the very things travel doctors say are best avoided on board the aircraft.

From the point of view of hygiene, aircraft food prepared or loaded in developing countries should carry the same health warnings as meals eaten out in the country of origin. Keep to the rules on page 35, taking special care to avoid salad, including lettuce and tomatoes.

Swollen ankles

This is common after long flights, with women being more affected than men. It can be helped by taking a walk every hour, which also reduces the risk of a blood clot developing in the legs – of especial importance in expectant mothers, the overweight and the elderly. If you have varicose veins or a history of leg thrombosis, wear elastic compression stockings during a flight.

Jet lag

All long flights, especially where sleep is lost, cause tiredness, as true for north-south flights as for transmeridian flights (east-west/west-east). After crossing time zones there is in addition a disturbance of the normal body rhythms including sleep patterns. This is largely responsible for the downside of intercontinental flying, jet lag, which for most people tends to be worse going from west to east.

Certain seasoned travellers affirm they have learnt the secret of dealing with this, but for most of us it has to be endured, and perhaps helped to a degree by a few commonsense precautions. These include trying to ensure two good nights' sleep before a long journey (beyond reach for all except the most highly organised), trying to sleep on the plane, avoiding caffeine and allowing yourself time to adjust on arrival (organisers of travel itineraries please note).

For a flight across five or more time zones, i.e. losing or gaining five hours or more, it is worth planning twenty-four hours in your new destination before any important activity or meeting.

Also, if your schedule allows, try to arrive as near as possible to your normal bedtime, and take a daytime flight.

Some experts claim that travelling east you should fly earlier in the day; and travelling west, later. Alternatively or in addition, try exposing yourself to bright daylight or sun early in the day after eastward flight, or at the end of the day in westward. This helps to adjust the body clock.

A natural drug called melatonin has been shown to reduce jet lag though it is not yet generally available. A suggested dose is 5mg taken in the evening for three to seven days after arrival at the destination.

Insomnia

Only the lucky few are able to sleep on a long flight, and then to appear annoyingly fresh and enthusiastic on the day of arrival at the other side of the world.

For some people lack of sleep during flight and/or for a few nights after arrival can be a serious nuisance. This is especially true for those with important engagements or whose transworld responsibilities involve frequent crossing and recrossing of time zones.

In such cases there is a place for the use of sleeping pills. The three golden rules are: use in the lowest dose which works; use for as few nights as possible; and choose a short-acting preparation with minimal after-effects. Current favourites are temazepam 10mg (Normison) or zopiclone 7.5mg (Zimovane). In this country, they all have to be prescribed by a doctor (see Appendix A).

Those unfit to fly

If in doubt about flying you should discuss this with your own doctor or the medical officer of the airline. If you have any serious condition be sure to notify the airline well in advance. Please see the list on page 21 for conditions prohibited or considered dangerous in the air.

Have children, will travel

For further tips on in-flight children see page 131.

Medical supplies in transit

Remember that anything placed in the aircraft hold is liable to freeze deeply. This means that any immunisations and insulin should be taken in your hand luggage, preferably in a vacuum flask containing a sealed ice pack.

Fear of flying

Although this is very common, it may become so severe that it overshadows your trip or makes you want to cancel the flight.

If the fear is specific to a particular route, or particular airline, then make arrangements which avoid these as far as possible. Sometimes discussing your fears with a friend or member of the family can help you to see it in perspective. For elderly travellers or those unfamiliar with flying it helps to arrive at the airport in plenty of time, so avoiding last-minute panic and hassle; or even do a trial run from home to check-in.

It is worth remembering that a crash or hijack is extremely rare and that even if there were three times more air accidents than at present, flying would still be considered safe.

If the problem still seems to be getting on top of you then British Airways put on a special seminar and flight from either Heathrow or Manchester. For details of this service, for which there is a charge, phone 0161–832 7972. You do not need to be booked on a BA flight.

SECTION 2

WHILE ABROAD

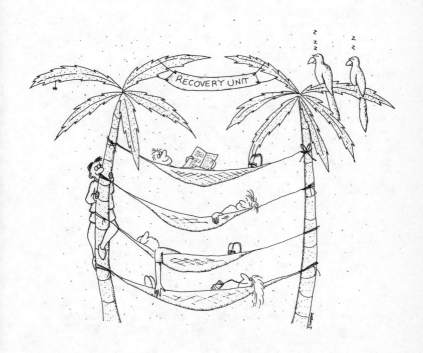

MAINTAINING GOOD HEALTH

PRECAUTIONS WITH FOOD

First the bad news: only a lucky few who visit or live in a developing country avoid getting stomach upsets or diarrhoea. Not surprisingly, fact and myth are often hopelessly mixed together on the vital topic of how to avoid Delhi Belly or Pharaoh's Revenge.

Now the good news: most bouts of diarrhoea clear up on their own after a few days.

In trying to avoid the runs it is helpful to steer a *middle path* between two extremes, typified on the one hand by the seasoned globetrotter with an apparently cast-iron stomach seizing any opportunity to savour the most exotic and ethnic fare; and on the other hand by the obsessional doomster who produces plastic mugs, disposable cutlery and paper napkins at the first sniff of indigenous food.

Of course by carefully preparing your own food at home you can eat virtually whatever you wish – and usually survive. Dangers mainly arise when eating out. Remember: restaurants are only as safe as the cleanliness of their kitchens and personal hygiene of their food handlers; in this respect budget travellers and five-star diplomats are more equal than they appear.

FOODS – SAFE AND UNSAFE

You probably won't come to grief if you stick with the following rules:

● **Okay**: *Food, recently cooked and served still hot*. Any food which has just been fried, or cooked at or above the normal boiling point of water for fifteen minutes or more, is perfectly safe. Fortunately much food comes into this category.

● **Okay**: *Fruit, either sterilised (see page 37) or carefully peeled (e.g. bananas)*.

● **Okay**: *Food (and drink) from sealed packs or cans.*

● **Avoid**: *Shellfish, lobsters, crabs or prawns.* In coastal areas known to be contaminated or where cholera is present these should be avoided altogether. Otherwise they can be eaten *if you are sure* they have been boiled for at least ten minutes (not easy to ascertain). *Sushi and raw fish – never eat.*

● **Avoid**: *Salads* unless carefully home-prepared.

● **Avoid**: *Uncooked vegetables or fruit* unless known to have been treated (see below). Wash fruit before slicing.

● **Avoid**: *Ice, icecream, milk, cheese and yoghurt* unless from a known safe, preferably pasteurised source.

● **Avoid**: *Food once hot, but served cold*, or on which flies may have settled.

● **Avoid**: *Food that has been reheated*, unless it is known to have been thoroughly recooked. This is especially important for rice.

● **Avoid**: *Eggs, unless cooked until the yolk goes solid.*

● **Avoid**: *Meat if any part of it remains pink.* Pork and beef may give you tapeworm, and chicken, Salmonella.

● **Avoid**: *Fancy, cold foods* which have involved much handling in their preparation.

● **Avoid**: *Table sauces*, as they are often diluted with unsafe water.

In summary: 'Cook it, peel it, clean it or leave it'.

PREPARING FOOD AT HOME

VEGETABLES should be *cleaned* of gross dirt, *peeled* where appropriate and then either *cooked* thoroughly, or *sterilised* (see page 37).

Consider *planting* your own vegetable garden, where you can grow leafy vegetables such as lettuce and spinach.

FRUIT should be *cleaned* of gross dirt, then *sterilised*, then *peeled*. Peeling an unwashed piece of fruit is an excellent way of transferring germs progressively inwards. Mango-eaters will understand this. Bananas are of course an exception.

MILK should be *boiled* for five minutes, then *cooled* immediately and kept *covered* and cool. A glass disc placed in the milk prevents it from boiling over and is worth buying before you go abroad.

STERILISATION. You can sterilise fruit and vegetables by adding tincture of iodine or water sterilisation tablets at three times the dose normally used for decontaminating water (see page 42). Then *soak* for at least twenty minutes, drain, or – better – rinse over with boiled water to remove the iodine and the taste of chlorine. Potassium permanganate is ineffective.

WASHING HANDS. Before eating or preparing food *wash your hands* thoroughly with soap. Young children's hands should be washed before meals and their nails *kept clean and short*.

SEPARATING COOKED FROM RAW FOOD. Don't allow fresh or cooked food to come into contact with raw, or contaminated food. This commonly occurs on surfaces, chopping boards and with knives. Beware of raw meat juice dripping in the fridge onto the shelf below.

LEFTOVER FOOD should either be *thrown away* or *refrigerated* immediately, and then *thoroughly recooked* within three days. Rice should be fully recooked and never simply reheated. Follow these rules strictly with food fed to babies.

FAILED FRIDGES. If the power supply fails disconnect the power supply, keep the door closed, cover the fridge with a soaked blanket and keep the blanket moist. Throw away any food that has returned to room temperature.

FOOD STORAGE. Protect your food from flies by netting or covers. A netted cupboard also protects from rodents. To keep ants away the legs of such cupboards can be placed in cups containing oil or salty water (the salt stops mosquitoes breeding).

DRAINAGE. Plates and cutlery should be *drained* in racks after washing.

COOKS, HOUSEBOYS AND AYAHS. Anyone you employ for

cooking should have *regular (six-monthly) stool tests* as cooks are commonly carriers of amoeba, Giardia or even typhoid. They should be encouraged to follow the same handwashing habits as you insist on for other family members. *Anyone with diarrhoea or a stomach upset should not be on cooking duty*.

LOCAL HOSPITALITY – BEWARE

At home, and to a large extent when eating in restaurants, you have control over what you eat. This is certainly not the case when invited to a meal by friends, the tribal chief, an important political leader or the local bishop. Unless you think fast you may have downed a whole range of suspect food (and drink) before you know it. As a guest your twin aim is to avoid offending both your host and your own digestion. Seasoned travellers can add their own suggestions to the advice given below:

• *Identify safe foods* and concentrate on those.

• *Identify and avoid foods* you consider suspect (including those you can't identify).

• *If in serious trouble*, play with and pretend to eat without actually doing so, or eat the smallest amounts possible.

• Explain *you are fasting* for religious or other reasons. Many cultures will readily understand this.

• Play the eccentric Brit who is quaintly apologetic for his strange food habits and weak digestion.

• Consider *saying 'grace'* before meals. It was originally intended for gratitude – and protection.

• *If in extremis* play the health card. Apologise that although you have always longed to eat raw camel's tail, your doctor has absolutely forbidden it.

A BALANCED DIET

As a general rule eat locally available food and enjoy special treats from home for special occasions. It is nearly always possible to eat a balanced diet overseas. One exception is when volunteers or off-beat travellers run out of money and stop buying adequate food.

The GOLDEN RULE OF NUTRITION is to maintain adequate, balanced intakes of the three main nutritional groups:

● *Carbohydrates* or energy foods (the staple food crops mentioned below).

● *Protein* or body-building foods from two or more sources such as meat, fish, eggs, lentils and grains. If you are going to be involved in any strenuous pursuits, especially mountaineering, eat plenty of protein, preferably meat.

● *Vitamins* – protective foods – especially vitamin A (green, leafy vegetables and yellow vegetables and fruit), B (whole grains and meat), and C (citrus fruit and other fresh fruit and vegetables). Vitamin D is largely made in the skin, when exposed to sunlight. Folate is present in fresh vegetables and liver, and is important for women who are either pregnant or planning pregnancy.

In addition *minerals*, especially iron, are also needed. Iron-rich foods include green leafy vegetables, eggs, fish and meat including liver. Calcium is especially needed by children, pregnant women and breastfeeding mothers. It is found mainly in milk and dairy products.

Each part of the world has a staple crop – either rice, wheat, maize, millet/sorghum, or roots and tubers, e.g. cassava, potatoes, sweet potatoes and yams.

As well as eating enough of these staples each day, which will be your main supply of energy (calories), you will need to add a protein source and locally available foods containing the three main vitamins. Only in exceptional circumstances will you need to take vitamin tablets if you eat correctly.

A reasonable rule of thumb is that a plateful of food containing three or more distinct colours (e.g. white/yellow for the staple food, green for vegetables containing vitamins A and C, and brown for meat containing protein, vitamin B and iron) is likely to be well balanced. Make sure however that vegetables are well- (but not over-) cooked and not eaten in the form of hastily prepared salads.

VEGETARIANS. It is possible, but in practice not always easy to be healthily vegetarian overseas. You must however ensure you are eating sufficient protein from several different sources. In practice vegetarians tend to lose weight more easily, especially in the Indian subcontinent, or after repeated stomach upsets. In these situations they are more likely to become anaemic, and deficient in folic acid, and should consider taking iron and folate supplements.

A sensible aim for all travellers is to maintain normal, i.e. correct body weight overseas. If overweight before departure try for an appropriate reduction before leaving and during the first few months abroad. In many developing-world cultures a *minor* degree of obesity is a sign that you are a person of substance or success, and small reserves may be useful if you fall sick, or find yourself in an appetite-depleting zone such as western Africa or monsoon Asia.

SAFE DRINKING

Although drinking mineral water in the UK may be more a cult than a necessity, obtaining sufficient clean water in the tropics is a major health issue. In the heat and humidity we need a huge supply of fluids, and a safe supply has to be set up.

Contaminated water causes many diseases. These include hepatitis, diarrhoeas and dysentery, typhoid, cholera, and polio. All these are caused by taking in organisms through the mouth, from sources contaminated by faeces. Some diseases, in particular bilharzia (schistosomiasis) are spread through the skin and are caught by swimming, splashing or washing in contaminated water.

WAYS OF MAKING WATER SAFE

Step 1: Identify a source

Find the nearest, cleanest source, such as a spring, a deep well, or a rainwater tank (except where roofs are painted with lead or made of thatch). If using tapped water identify where it comes from and make sure pipes and joints are sound. Hot tap water left to cool is a useful source in a hotel. Treat notices claiming all drinking water is boiled, with extreme caution. Beware of shallow tube wells which are often contaminated. An ideal water supply is cool, clear and odourless.

Step 2: If cloudy, let it stand

Then decant it, or filter it through a cloth, fine gauze or Millbank Bag.

Step 3: Sterilise it

There are three possible ways of ridding water of germs:

(a) Boiling:

This is the most reliable method and kills all organisms including viruses and amoebic cysts. Unless your water is known to be from a safe source *or* there is a serious lack of fuel, boiling is the method of choice.

Experts disagree about the exact length of time needed. A good rule of thumb is to boil (a rolling boil) for five minutes plus one minute extra for every 1,000 metres (3,000 feet) you are above sea level. Boiling water for twenty minutes is unnecessary and a waste of natural resources.

After boiling let the water cool and stand for a few hours to improve the taste.

When making hot drinks at home such as tea and coffee remember to let the water boil for five minutes. This means avoiding electric kettles which switch themselves off on boiling.

Use boiled water for cleaning your teeth, keeping a separate supply in the bathroom. In an emergency just use toothpaste and saliva.

(b) Filtering:

Water is filtered for one of two reasons:

● To remove suspended material prior to boiling (see step 2 above).

● As a convenient alternative to boiling, and when there is a shortage of fuel or time.

Water should *not* be filtered after it has been boiled, despite some fondly-held traditions. It risks recontamination, and is the equivalent of 'washing whiter with Persil', and then finishing the job off with ordinary soap.

The best filters, used correctly and cleaned regularly, are almost as reliable as boiling, though some viruses may not be excluded.

Water passes through a filter either by gravity, or through an attached pump, or direct from a tap through a special attachment.

There are two recommended materials used for filtration:

● *Ceramic* filters, using porcelain 'candles'. The pore size should be as small as possible, ideally 0.5µ, and the filter impregnated with silver which kills most micro-organisms. Katadyne is a well-known brand. Ceramic filters are suitable for home use.

● *Iodine resin* filters. Contact with iodine kills micro-organisms, and releases a low level of iodine for continuing disinfection. These are ideal when on the road (see page 44 for suggested models).

All filters need to be carefully maintained according to the manufacturer's instructions. Ceramic candles should be regularly cleaned, handled with care and checked for any breaks or cracks which will render them useless. They can be boiled unless impregnated with silver.

(c) Disinfecting:

This is slightly less reliable than boiling and the best filtering.

Chlorine-based disinfectants can be used. These kill most organisms but not amoebic cysts nor the hepatitis A virus. Puritabs and Steritabs are well-known brands. Household bleach can also be used: add two drops of a 5–6% solution of available chlorine to one litre, or add eight drops of a 1% solution. (One drop is about 0.05ml.) The water should smell and taste faintly of chlorine.

Iodine is rather more effective, killing most organisms and having some action on amoebic cysts. Buy Potable Aqua tablets and dissolve one in a litre of water, or as per manufacturer's instructions. An alternative is to add five drops of 2% tincture of iodine (2% is the normal concentration) to one litre of water. It is probably better not to use iodine long-term and to use sparingly during pregnancy or if you suffer from thyroid problems.

You can double all the above doses in the short term if the water is cloudy.

After adding the tablets or solution to the water allow to stand for twenty to thirty minutes at normal room temperatures, or for one to two hours if very cold.

Step 4: Storing water

Boiled water should ideally be stored in the container in which it was boiled. Alternatively it can be poured into a previously sterilised narrow-necked earthenware jar, and placed on a clean, dry surface. The jar will need careful and regular cleaning and should be kept covered. No one should be allowed to dip into it.

Many expatriates keep two large kettles, using each in turn first to boil, then to store. In this way there is a constant supply of cool, boiled water.

Water is best removed from its storage container through a tap or spout. Dippers are unsafe as they frequently get left on the floor and contaminate the whole supply. A good rule is 'Tap or tip, don't dip'.

SAFE FLUIDS – ON THE ROAD

When on the road or in difficult conditions boiling or filtering is not always possible. Many cases of diarrhoea are caused by thirsty travellers drinking what's offered and hoping for the best.

Here are some suggestions:

● Keep to *hot* drinks. Tea and coffee are usually safe, the milk usually being added to the brew and boiled up together. Try to avoid any cup that is obviously cracked or has just been swilled out with dirty water. In some countries, it is cultural to swill out cups and rice bowls with boiling tea and pour them out.

• Keep to *carbonated* soft drinks from bottles with metal tops from reputable firms. Such drinks are usually clean and their slight acidity kills some organisms. Avoid bottles with loose or suspect tops, and soda or mineral water bottles whose contents may have been replenished from a tap.

Bottles of mineral water are now available in many countries. Although some of them are undoubtedly clean and genuine, others definitely are not. It takes an experienced eye to tell them apart. *Only use those with unbroken seals*.

Make sure all soft-drink bottles are opened in your presence. If drinking straight from the bottle, clean the rim with care as it may have been resting in water to keep cool.

• Always carry a *vacuum* flask or other container with a clean drink of your choice.

• Always have some *water sterilising tablets* with you. They should be dry and reasonably fresh. (Yellowing tablets are losing their potency.)

• If using a *plastic water bottle* for travelling or trekking, allow boiled water to cool first before pouring it into the bottle, otherwise the taste will be nauseating.

• Carry a small, portable *water filter* such as a Travel Well, Trekker Travel Well, Travel Cup or Pentapure. These are able to filter sufficient water for one or two people. Check the specifications from one of the suppliers in Appendix C to make sure it exactly fits your needs.

• *Avoid ice*. Freezing does not kill organisms and ice often comes from an impure source.

• *Avoid milk* unless just boiled.

• *Avoid* excessive *alcohol*. It disinhibits, dehydrates and does not sterilise, making it a low entry on the tropical drinks hit parade.

SWIMMING

Avoid swimming in contaminated lakes, seas, rivers or ponds. Not only are you likely to take in water, but you can catch skin infections. In many areas of Africa, east Asia and parts of South America, bilharzia is a risk (see pages 162–5). Crocodiles and sharks are not reported to have lost their appetites.

Avoid swimming on *beaches* near to cities if there is a known cholera outbreak, or where the sea is obviously polluted.

Swimming pools which smell of chlorine are generally considered safe.

When babies and very young children swim or have a bath they often take in water. Make the bath as hot as possible, then let it cool to the right temperature for bathing.

HYGIENE AT HOME

You can prevent most illnesses in the tropics by setting up an appropriate lifestyle, avoiding malaria and taking care with food and water.

Clean personal and domestic habits also have an important part to play.

In hot countries it is essential to *wash* frequently, not only because of the heat and dust but also because of the great number of germs which find your body surface a cosy environment. When the weather is hot, try to wash twice daily, at least once with soap, preferably using a shower. This will help to prevent boils and skin infections. Water supply allowing, leave the shower to run briefly before getting under it, and try to avoid the water getting into your mouth. To reduce the likelihood of getting worms, keep your fingernails clean and short and wear shoes when outside the house.

You should change your *clothes* regularly and keep them well-laundered. This especially goes for underwear and socks.

You should dry clothes on a line, not the ground, and in areas where the tumbu fly is found (see page 111), you should dry them inside the house *or* iron them; hot-iron all clothes which may touch the skin: this should include non-disposable nappies and underclothes.

It is worth being very careful with *domestic* hygiene. Scraps of food left around quickly decompose or attract insects and animals. Take care that the house is swept regularly and the *kitchen* is kept really clean. Make sure that any rag used for the floor is both separate and obviously different from any cloth used for wiping tables (and explain this carefully to anyone who works for you).

Toilets, whatever their type, easily attract flies and you will need to have them regularly cleaned, especially where children are using them. If you are building a latrine it should be twenty metres or more from any water source or river, and on a lower level. It should have a tight-fitting lid and ideally be based on a 'VIP' pit-latrine model.

Keep the *surrounds* of the house or camp clean, free from standing water (to reduce malarial risk) and free from thick or high vegetation (to reduce the risk of snakes entering). Make sure you have a good *drainage system* for household water, keeping soakaways clean and deslimed. Any *rainwater tank* needs to be well maintained, have a tight-fitting lid to prevent mosquitoes from breeding, and be allowed to wash through at the start of the rainy season. Keep your *windows*, doors and screening in a good state of repair to reduce the number of insects (especially mosquitoes) entering the house.

House temperature can be kept lower by making sure all outer walls are pale or white, and that you use a non-heat-absorbing roofing material. If this is not possible paint the roof white. Other measures which will keep the house cool are over-hanging eaves, and insulating the roof by placing a layer of bamboo, grasses or thatch on top. Tall rooms with openings near the top and with large lower windows set opposite each other help air-flow.

You can keep *flies* to the minimum by good household hygiene, screening, swatting and the use of insecticides and fly-traps. Pyrethroid insecticides are effective against *cockroaches*. *Ants* should be killed with an appropriate antkiller before they get established, otherwise it will be ants and marmalade for breakfast. Food should always be carefully stored, covered or screened so that no insect or animal can touch it.

Household rubbish needs to be appropriately disposed of. In rural areas you can separate it into material suitable for burning, composting and burial. Any rubbish dump, either household or communal, needs to be deep, a good distance from the house and kept covered with earth so that animals and children don't further scatter the contents. Rubbish awaiting disposal should be stored in a strong container, kept raised off the ground and have its lid secured for protection against raiding animals.

Household pets can easily introduce diseases into the house. Take special care with dogs which will need to be restricted in where they roam, be kept clean, be carefully housetrained, have deworming medicine every six months, and from the age of three months be kept up-to-date with their rabies injections. Three-yearly boosters of a live attenuated vaccine are normally used which if not available where you live can be brought out from the UK. Dogs should not be 'kissed' and after petting them or playing with them you should wash your hands (and those of your children).

Finally if you employ a *house servant* who is not used to working

It wasn't like this in Basildon!

with expatriates explain basic rules of hygiene. This, along with a medical check and regular stool test will help to keep the whole household more healthy.

DEALING WITH DIARRHOEA
'Travel broadens the mind but loosens the bowel'

For most travellers in developing countries diarrhoea is not a matter of If, but of When. This section which is therefore quite detailed, aims to help you deal with the almost inevitable, and to recognise and treat the more serious. It covers the following:

- What are the main types of diarrhoea?
- Action plan for acute diarrhoea
- Treatment of persistent diarrhoea
- Amoebic infection
- Giardiasis
- Antibiotics to prevent traveller's diarrhoea
- Diarrhoea in the local population
- Cholera
- Typhoid

Prevention of diarrhoea through water and food hygiene is dealt with separately (see pages 35–48)

WHAT ARE THE MAIN TYPES OF DIARRHOEA?

Although more than one hundred organisms are known to cause diarrhoea, experienced travellers find it helpful to divide The Runs into one of three main types:

1. *Acute watery diarrhoea* lasting a few days, with little or no fever, is the commonest form. Four out of five cases are caused by either E. coli, Campylobacter, Shigella or Salmonella. Viruses account for most of the remainder. Malaria can sometimes cause diarrhoea (see figure on page 53).

Cholera, rare in expatriates, can cause extremely severe, almost continuous watery diarrhoea (see below).

2. *Acute diarrhoea with blood* (usually known as *dysentery*). There are two common types:

● In *bacillary* dysentery (caused by Shigella) there is profuse bloody diarrhoea usually with mucus (often twelve or more stools in twenty-four hours) with severe straining, griping and a feeling of doom. Fever is present.

● With acute *amoebic* dysentery the symptoms are usually less severe, with little or no fever and rarely more than six to twelve stools in twenty-four hours.

Other organisms can cause blood in the stools including Campylobacter (similar though usually less severe than bacillary dysentery), typhoid (see below), and schistosomiasis (see page 162).

3. *Chronic diarrhoea* (lasting seven days or more). Any of the above can persist. However chronic diarrhoea is often caused by amoeba or Giardia (see below and figure on page 53).

ACTION PLAN FOR ACUTE DIARRHOEA

Here are four broad categories. Treat according to which you most obviously come under:

(a) Mild symptoms

You have symptoms which do not interfere with normal activities; you feel generally well. Treatment: keep up fluid intake and reduce the amount of food you eat. (Children should still be fed.)

(b) Moderate symptoms

Your symptoms threaten normal activities or travel; you feel reasonably well, and have no fever or dysentery.

Treatment: as in (a) above plus the following:

● loperamide 2mg tablets (Imodium) two together then one every four hours until symptoms improve.

● ciprofloxacin 250mg tablets two together as a single dose.

(c) More severe symptoms

You are unable to carry out normal activities, feel unwell but have no dysentery and only little or no fever.

Treatment: as (b) above except continue ciprofloxacin 250mg tablets two daily for three days.

(d) Dysentery

You have blood in your stool and/or fever and feel unwell, possibly seriously so. Treatment: as (c) above, but continue ciprofloxacin 250mg two daily for five days. (See also Amoebiasis on page 52.) Consider seeing a doctor.

Treatment for children

Keeping up fluids is by far the most important treatment (see below). Drugs are less important and should not normally be used as a home remedy in children under 4 years of age.

For children 4 and over with more severe symptoms you can use the following:

● loperamide (Imodium) as a blocking agent in doses four times a day for a twenty-four hour period as follows: age 4–8: 1mg; age 9–12: 2mg dose. Loperamide comes both as tablets and as a liquid suspension.

● antibiotics as follows: either cotrimoxazole, or erythromycin or furazolidone (not available in UK) as per doctor's or manufacturer's dosages.

Treatment with these antibiotics in most parts of the world will be rather less effective than the ciprofloxacin used for adults. This is because of widespread drug resistance to those antibiotics which are safe in children.

Treatment for pregnant women

Pregnant women should generally use rehydration only and avoid drugs unless seriously ill.

Keeping up fluids in diarrhoea

You can use any appropriate non-alcoholic or non-milk based fluid, such as soft drinks (e.g. Sprite, 7-Up), weak tea or light soup. A simple method is to buy packets of Oral Rehydration

Salts (ORS) and mix them with water as per instructions. Common brands are Dioralyte, Rehydrat or other sachets recommended by the World Health Organisation (WHO).

It is also possible to make your own mixture. The methods and amounts recommended vary considerably. Currently the WHO in a leaflet for travellers produced in June 1991 recommends mixing six level teaspoons of sugar with one level teaspoon of salt in one litre of safe, preferably boiled drinking water. Children under 2 are spooned one quarter to one half cup after each stool, those from 2 years to 10 sip half to one cup per stool, older children and adults as much as they require, usually at least one cup per stool. Breastfed children should continue to receive breastmilk.

If signs of dehydration occur, e.g. dry lips and tongue, inelastic skin, absent or highly concentrated urine, double the amount until these symptoms disappear. If vomiting also occurs sips should be taken more slowly, until the nausea improves.

When to see a doctor

You should seek further help under the following situations:

• your symptoms do not largely subside within forty-eight hours;

• you are seriously ill;

• you have uncontrollable vomiting and/or marked abdominal pain;

• you (or your children) are severely dehydrated.

Don't forget that diarrhoea may mean you have malaria. If in doubt get a blood smear.

TREATMENT OF CHRONIC (PERSISTENT) DIARRHOEA

Diarrhoea lasting seven days or more (group 3, p. 49) tends to cause much concern and discussion amongst travellers. Before treating it, or imagining a giant amoeba eating away at your intestines, it is worth trying to identify the cause. The two ways are:

• A stool test. Take a fresh stool in a labelled, waterproof container to a reliable laboratory and await the result. If the first is negative arrange two further tests.

● Inspired guesswork. If a stool test is negative, impossible to arrange or thought to be unreliable you will need to try and match cause to symptoms according to the descriptions below:

Amoebiasis

This is common in most developing countries. *Symptoms* include blood and mucus in the stool, but these are often over-looked. Loose bowels may alternate with constipation: lower abdominal pain is common. There may be some weight loss. Chronic sufferers often become ill-tempered and introverted.

Occasionally amoebas travel upstream to the liver causing amoebic hepatitis or an abscess. Suspect this if you develop a fever (often, but not always high or 'swinging') or pain in the upper right part of the abdomen or under the right rib cage. This must be treated urgently.

Treatment of amoebiasis is as follows: tinidazole 500mg (Fasigyn) four together after food on three successive evenings, *or* metronidazole 400mg (Flagyl) five together after food on three successive evenings, or two, three times a day for five days. If you suspect liver involvement take metronidazole 400mg tablets, two, three times a day for ten days. These drugs can make you feel ill, often causing headache, nausea and a conviction that the treatment is worse than the cure. Alcohol should be strictly avoided as it worsens the side-effects. Avoid in pregnancy.

After finishing your course of Fasigyn or Flagyl, you should ideally take diloxanide 500mg (Furamide) one, three times a day for ten days (this kills the amoebic cysts).

It is unwise to take *repeated* courses of amoeba treatment unless there is evidence on a fresh stool test of active motile forms (trophozoites), or you have very typical symptoms.

Amoebas are sometimes overlooked: they are often also unfairly blamed for a variety of afflictions. An obsession with amoeba is as common as an infection, and there comes a time when a self-imposed ban on 'The Amoebes', both in conversation and in letters home, is the most appropriate action.

Giardiasis

This is also common in many areas of the tropics and within the Russian Federation. *Symptoms* include offensive wind and diarrhoea, loss of appetite, nausea and heartburn. It sometimes leads to milk (lactose) intolerance (see below).

Treatment is as follows: *either* tinidazole 500mg (Fasigyn) four together after food, repeat same dose in two weeks, *or* metronidazole 400mg (Flagyl) five tablets together (2gm) daily after food, for three days.

Avoid alcohol while on treatment, and again be warned of the side-effects.

Giardiasis and some other bowel infections can lead on to *lactose (milk) intolerance*, which is one cause of persistent diarrhoea and flatulence. One way of telling whether you

FLOW CHART FOR PERSISTENT OR RECURRENT DIARRHOEA (seven days or longer)

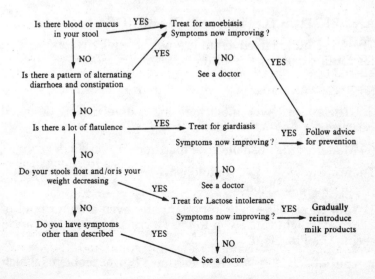

have this is to drink one to two pints of boiled milk and see if your symptoms of diarrhoea and flatulence obviously worsen over the following few hours. If they do, consider avoiding all dairy products for a period of three months, then gradually reintroducing them.

Sometimes repeated bowel infections, including Giardia, cause the lining of the small intestine to be less efficient in absorbing food. This is known as *tropical malabsorption*. Typical symptoms are floating, frothy stools, loss of weight, thinning muscles, and decreasing energy. This condition is especially seen in those living or budget travelling in south Asia. If you suspect this you must see a doctor.

A variety of other germs can cause persistent diarrhoea, including some which first cause acute symptoms and then remain as unwelcome visitors. They cannot be identified by guesswork and most will eventually disappear on their own. If you have had repeated or persistent bouts of diarrhoea you should have a stool test on your return home, and see a doctor with experience in travel medicine. Occasionally non-tropical bowel problems first start in the tropics or after returning home, meaning *you should always report any persisting symptoms*.

ANTIBIOTICS TO PREVENT DIARRHOEA

These are quite effective but are not generally recommended for routine use because of the following reasons:

(a) Their widespread use will lead to drug resistance.

(b) There are fewer medicines in reserve if you do need treatment.

(c) Modern drugs usually cure diarrhoea if you do develop it.

There are however two situations where it is worth considering preventative antibiotics:

1. Your trip is especially important and even a minor bout of diarrhoea might cause you to miss a crucial journey or cancel seeing the President.

2. Your health is indifferent, you have bowel problems which

could be worsened by diarrhoea, you consider yourself to be frail or elderly.

In these cases the best drugs to prevent diarrhoea are either ciprofloxacin 500mg daily, norfloxacin 400mg daily, ofloxacin 300mg daily, starting each twenty-four hours before leaving, continuing for forty-eight hours after returning, and restricting the total length of treatment to no longer than fourteen days.

Slightly less effective alternatives are trimethoprim 200mg daily or doxycycline 100mg daily, each of which can be taken for longer. None of these should be used in pregnancy.

DIARRHOEA IN THE LOCAL POPULATION

It is likely that diarrhoea will be one of the commonest causes of severe illness and death amongst the children in the area where you are living. You should become familiar with the nationally recommended or local method of making oral rehydration solution (ORS) so that you can use and demonstrate this when you are consulted by your neighbours.

CHOLERA

Extent: there were more reported cases of cholera in 1991 than in the whole of the previous ten years, and numbers remain high. There continue to be outbreaks in many countries of South and Central America, tropical Africa and Asia. A virulent strain, 0139 or Bengal cholera, is spreading from south Asia.

Cause: cholera is a disease of poverty and is most common in areas of social and economic deprivation or civil war. It is spread by faecal contamination of water supplies and food, in particular fish and shellfish, raw fruit and vegetables. The germ which causes it is known as Vibrio cholerae.

Risk and prevention: the risk to travellers is very low and it can be prevented by taking care with personal hygiene and by following strict rules on drinking water and food preparation (see pages 35–44). If travelling with a family or leading a group make sure everyone knows and obeys basic rules of hygiene.

A cholera vaccine is available and gives about 50% protection to most strains but none to Bengal cholera. Although it is not currently recommended for use by the World Health Organisation there may be a case for using this if working or travelling in areas where a cholera epidemic is occurring (see page 218). The full course is two, followed by a booster dose after six months from a reliable health facility. An oral vaccine is currently being tested. Remember that care with food and water is of far greater importance than the use of the vaccine, and if you are immunised you should not be lulled into a false sense of security.

Symptoms: although most cases of cholera cause nothing more than mild diarrhoea, typical life-threatening episodes have to be recognised and treated urgently as they can cause death from dehydration within just a few hours. They usually start with massive, often continuous watery diarrhoea, often resembling rice water. There is commonly vomiting, but abdominal pain is usually mild. Dehydration occurs rapidly.

Treatment: this depends on the use of adequate amounts of oral rehydration solution. You can either use packets of ORS made up with boiled water or make your own by mixing six level teaspoons of sugar and one level teaspoon of salt to one litre of boiled water and drinking one to two cups per stool (see also page 51). Vomiting is best treated by drinking: start with small amounts at a time and increase as rapidly as possible. Slow sipping often eases the nausea.

Also take doxycycline tabs 100mg, two together for three days (total six). One trade name is Vibramycin. If you are going to an area where a cholera outbreak is occurring consider taking two courses (twelve) with you. Most GPs will prescribe these, though you may have to pay for them.

Even in an epidemic area you are in fact very unlikely to get cholera if you take sensible precautions. You may however get other forms of diarrhoea which you should manage according to the guidelines given. The main treatment of all forms of acute diarrhoea, including cholera, is oral rehydration solution.

If your symptoms or those of your colleague suggest cholera you should follow this procedure:

● Start oral rehydration solution at once and continue until the diarrhoea has improved and a good output of urine is produced.

• Take doxycycline as recommended above.

• See a doctor or reliable health worker as soon as possible.

Please also see Appendix F, pages 218–19.

TYPHOID (Enteric fever)

Symptoms: diarrhoea may occur with typhoid in the later stages (especially if untreated) but constipation and cough are often present early. A typical attack of typhoid causes a severe and worsening illness, head and body ache, a temperature which rises higher each day, with your pulse staying relatively slow, often at about eighty beats per minute. After one or two weeks diarrhoea usually develops, often with blood, offensive breath, and abdominal pain.

If you have been immunised against typhoid, symptoms may be less severe and harder to tell apart from other conditions. Typhoid may occasionally be the cause of persistent or inter-mittent diarrhoea, low-grade fever or worsening health.

The best treatment for those aged 18 and over is ciprofloxacin 500–750mg twice daily for ten to fourteen days. An alternative is chloramphenicol 500mg four times daily for two weeks, but this is not always effective especially in Asia. These are not appropriate in pregnancy.

Even after typhoid is apparently cured it is still possible to be a carrier. Anyone preparing or cooking food who may have had typhoid should first have a negative stool test.

Please also see Appendix F, pages 227–8.

DEFEATING MALARIA

Please read this section carefully before you go overseas.

In many developing countries malaria is the most important and most serious disease you are likely to face. It is therefore worth being extremely careful about *preventing* it, and being

Good Health, Good Travel

World Mosquito Conference 1995: maximising impact

well informed about how to recognise and *treat* it. Ways of doing this are described below and you will need to take various supplies with you. These must include both antimalarial tablets as well as other items to prevent you from being bitten. Make sure you are well informed, well prepared and well stocked before leaving home.

WHERE IS MALARIA FOUND?

At the present time malaria is found in at least 105 countries and nearly two billion people are at risk (see map, opposite). Malaria is thought to kill over one million children per year in Africa alone.

Within individual countries malaria may be common in some areas, absent in others. It is rarely found above about 2,000 metres (about 6,500 feet). Some cities within malarious areas may be virtually free while nearby forested areas or irrigated fields may be badly affected. In some countries, e.g. parts of lowland tropical Africa, malaria is found throughout the year whilst in other areas, e.g. some highland areas of Africa and in monsoon Asia, malaria tends to be more seasonal.

In many areas malaria is becoming both more common and more difficult to treat. There are several reasons for this: mosquitoes are becoming resistant to insecticides, Plasmodium

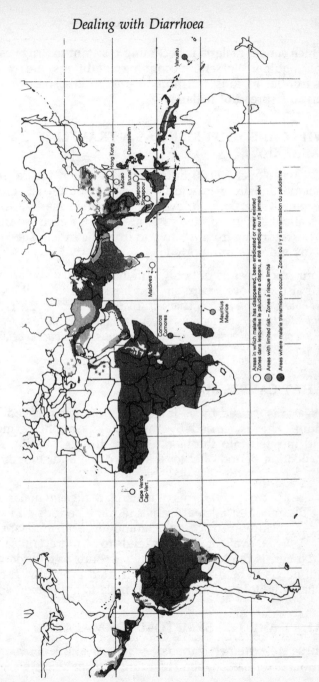

Areas where malaria is found (WHO 1991)

○ Areas in which malaria has disappeared, been eradicated or never existed
Zones dans lesquelles le paludisme a disparu, a été éradiqué ou n'a jamais sévi

◐ Areas with limited risk – Zones à risque limité

● Areas where malaria transmission occurs – Zones où il y a transmission du paludisme

Vanuatu

Hong Kong
Macao
Brunei Darussalam
Singapore
Singapour

Maldives

Comoros
Comores

Mauritius
Maurice

Cape Verde
Cap-Vert

which causes malaria is becoming resistant to drugs especially chloroquine. Worsening economic conditions, the opening up of frontier regions and human migration also encourage the onward spread of malaria.

WHAT ARE YOUR RISKS AS A TRAVELLER OR EXPATRIATE?

Each year over 30,000 European and American travellers get malaria, mostly in tropical Africa and south-east Asia. Some become seriously ill, a few (usually unnecessarily) die. In the UK about 2,000 imported cases are reported each year mostly in those returning from Africa and from the Indian subcontinent; many more go unreported.

Your risk depends not only on which *country* you are visiting, but also on your *occupation* and *lifestyle*. Above all it depends on *how well you protect yourself. By taking a few simple precautions and following them rigorously, you are much less likely to get malaria. If you start treatment as soon as suspicious symptoms develop you are very unlikely to become seriously ill.*

WHAT CAUSES MALARIA?

Malaria is caused by a single-celled organism called Plasmodium. This is carried by the female Anopheles mosquito, and injected into the blood stream through a bite. After an incubation period of at least seven days, and sometimes very much longer, the disease develops.

There are two main forms of malaria. *Malignant* malaria caused by Plasmodium falciparum is the more serious and in many areas, including Africa, the commoner. *Benign* malaria caused by P. vivax, ovale or malariae tends to be more a nuisance than a danger, is rarely fatal, usually responds to chloroquine, but still needs to be diagnosed and treated promptly. It can only reliably be told from falciparum malaria by a blood smear.

WHAT ARE THE SYMPTOMS OF MALARIA?

These are extremely variable. A 'typical' attack of malaria starts with a *cold* phase, when shivering and shaking start suddenly and last up to one hour. This is followed by a *hot dry phase*, lasting two to six hours when the temperature may rise up to 40°C (104°F), there is headache, pains in the joints and often vomiting and diarrhoea. Finally comes the hot wet phase, lasting two to four hours when the patient sweats profusely and then feels better.

Left untreated these phases tend to recur every two days (tertian fever – P. falciparum, vivax or ovale) or much more rarely every three days (quartan fever – P. malariae).

However most attacks of malaria do not follow these phases, especially if you are taking antimalarials. Malignant malaria especially, may cause a variety of symptoms including continuous or more often irregular fever. Malaria in children under three months may not cause fever at all.

This means that malaria can mimic a whole range of illnesses. Experienced hands learn to recognise them. Mild fever, headache, a bout of vomiting and diarrhoea, or simply feeling off-colour may indicate an attack. A severe cold, an operation, and a time of stress or exhaustion may cause a relapse and bring out symptoms. The strain of bringing a family, or just yourself, back to the UK may trigger an attack.

Malignant malaria if not treated early can progress rapidly and cause serious illness within hours. Cerebral malaria affects the brain and may cause fits and fluctuating levels of consciousness

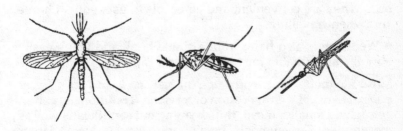

Anopheles mosquito (female 4–6mm long)

before leading to coma and death. Danger signs, usually obvious, include drowsiness, confusion, absent urine, shortness of breath, jaundice and persistent fever. Repeated attacks of malaria may lead to exhaustion and contribute towards depression. The spleen may enlarge and anaemia may develop.

HOW CAN YOU AVOID MALARIA?

There are two main ways – AVOIDING MOSQUITO BITES AND TAKING PROPHYLACTICS.

Avoiding bites

Here are some ways of reducing the risk:

1. Sleep under a mosquito net (bed net)

Use these in areas where malaria is known to occur, even if there don't seem to be many mosquitoes. One bite is enough to cause infection, especially in parts of Africa because so many mosquitoes are carriers. Check there are no holes in the net.

Of course mosquito nets also help to protect against several other insect-borne diseases. Nets come in various shapes:

● Rectangular nets are traditional. They are suspended at four corners and are the standard nets used in many homes and guest houses. They come in double, single and cot size.

● Bell nets are suspended on a hoop above the bed and hang from a single hook in the ceiling. These nets are now commonly made in one size which can be used for cots, single or double beds. They are convenient and agreeable to use, both at home and when travelling.

● Wedge nets also hang from a single hook and being easily portable are suitable for travelling and camping.

Mosquito nets come with *different size mesh* and in *different materials* – usually either cotton or terylene. Traditionally cotton nets have a smaller mesh, thus keeping out sandflies as well as mosquitoes. Terylene nets, being hotter, tend to have a larger mesh; they are also more durable than cotton.

The *most effective and convenient net* to take with you is usually a large mesh bell net soaked in permethrin or deltamethrin, or a new substance lambdacyhalothrin (trade name, Icon). Permethrin is an insecticide which kills and repels mosquitoes (and other biting insects) and nets soaked in it are far more effective than standard nets and can safely be left to hang loose (ideally right down to the floor), without being tucked in. They also act as mosquito killers, so reducing the number of flying insects in the house. Remember however to resoak them at least every six months and whenever they are washed. Instructions on how to do this come with the permethrin solution. Icon lasts for at least one year, but its use is otherwise similar.

Before you take up an overseas posting find out if an appropriate net is provided or available locally and if not take one with you, along with sufficient permethrin for resoaking, if you are going for more than six months.

2. Cover your skin

Mosquitoes commonly bite at sunset then continue late into the night – skilfully co-ordinating their day's work with your evening's pleasure and arriving as unwelcome intruders at the very time you want to relax outside. They also favour dawn, so affecting the early risers.

Mosquitoes will go for any part of the body but tend to specialise in wrist and face, ankles and feet (catching you unawares under the table). Climate allowing, wear long cotton sleeves and long trousers if you go out in the evening, preferably of light-coloured material. Remember that a determined mosquito can bite through socks or two pairs of tights, which means that cover alone is not always enough.

3. Use an insect repellent

In order to be effective this must contain either the active ingredient DEET (diethyl-toluamide), dimethyl phthalate, or 'natural' lemon eucalyptus oil. Citronella-based products are probably less effective. Repellents can be applied in various ways: direct to the skin, as a cream, gel, stick, roll-on or spray. They last up to about four hours and are reasonably effective, but may leave an unpleasant sticky feeling to the skin. Autan and Jungle formula are well-known brands containing DEET. Mosiguard Naturel is eucalyptus based.

For young children use concentrations of DEET below 35%. Do not use at all in babies. Do not apply to the lips or eyelids. DEET tends to destroy plastic and nail varnish. In the rare case of an allergic reaction, e.g. itching, swelling, blistering, stop using it immediately, and take an antihistamine.

4. Soak or spray your clothes

You have two choices:

(a) *Using DEET* you can soak cotton garments in a solution of 30ml of DEET added to 250ml of water.

Ankle- and wrist-bands can also be pre-soaked in permethrin. A well-known brand is Mosiguard. Clothes and bands should be kept in a sealed container when not being used as this increases their useful life to about 120 hours before needing a resoak.

Use DEET-soaked clothing with caution in children, and do not use with babies.

(b) *Permethrin*. You can soak clothes in permethrin using the solution according to manufacturer's instructions, usually at 0.2gm per square metre of material. Alternatively you can make up a solution and spray clothing. Permethrin spray though licensed in the USA is not yet available in the UK, though you can make up your own using a spray bottle.

Remember that DEET repels mosquitoes but does not necessarily kill them; permethrin kills but does not necessarily repel them.

Here are some suggestions for areas where there is a severe mosquito or insect nuisance:

• When outside in the evening wear appropriate clothing, apply a DEET-based insect repellent, and wear wrist-bands and ankle-bands or pre-soaked socks.

• Inside the house use permethrin-impregnated bed nets (and curtains).

• When walking outside in highly affected areas, including trekking in tick- and leech- infested country, use DEET insect repellent on the skin and permethrin-soaked clothing.

Those who are likely to be outside after sunset in malarious areas are strongly recommended to apply insect repellent thoroughly to all exposed areas of the skin.

5. Screen your room

In areas with many mosquitoes you can fix fine metal screening to your windows and doors, and make sure they are kept closed from about two hours before sunset to well after sunrise. Check for any holes or gaps in the screening. The netting should have six or seven threads per centimetre width.

6. Use an aerosol or flit gun

These, also known as knock-down sprays, contain a pyrethroid insecticide and can be used in the house every evening. Spray sleeping areas, being careful to include dark corners, hidden areas behind cupboards, under beds and most important of all the bath or shower room. These sprays do not necessarily kill mosquitoes that arrive after you have finished spraying, i.e. they have little 'residual' effect.

7. Other night-time precautions

Mosquito coils can be burned. They are effective and their vapour is safe. Under a fan or in a breeze they may run out before dawn. They are available cheaply in many tropical countries, but beware of fake products.

Vapourising mats. A tablet of pyrethroid insecticide is placed on a mains-operated heating plate. These are available in many countries but depend on a reliable night-time electricity supply, unless you buy a battery-operated model or improvise your own from a 12-volt battery. They are thought to be more effective than coils.

Sleeping under a ceiling fan or in an air-conditioned room keeps mosquitoes at bay – until the electricity goes off.

'Buzzers' have no effect on mosquitoes.

8. Deal with the source

Try to eliminate breeding sites near the house. These include thick vegetation, ponds, areas of stagnant water including animal hoofprints, rainwater tanks with poorly fitting lids, the axils of leaves, pots on the verandah and the tops of bamboo canes. Mosquitoes can fly at least a mile, but eliminating the breeding sites within the immediate area of the house reduces the number.

Make sure that open water tanks are screened, using the same mesh size as for house screening.

Arrange for the government spraying team to visit your area. Consider stocking nearby ponds or paddyfields with larvicidal fish, e.g. guppy, or procuring polystyrene beads to put into wet pits and pit latrines.

Taking prophylactics (antimalarials) to prevent malaria

If you take the *correct* pills *without missing doses* you are much less likely to get malaria, and even if you do, research has shown *it is likely to be less severe* and will allow you longer time to receive proper treatment. Research also indicates that the majority of those insisting they have taken their antimalarials have in fact forgotten a significant number of doses.

Gulliver, in his travels to Lilliput, was surprised to discover that civil war started over whether to open a boiled egg at the large end or the small end. Most expatriates soon find that the answer as to which is the best antimalarial is an equally divisive issue, the European, the Brit and the North American rarely agreeing. The advice in this book follows recommendations from the Malaria Reference Laboratory in London (1995), and the World Health Organisation (1994).

Whichever antimalarial you take follow these rules:

• Choose the recommended regime before you leave and do not change or stop unless there is a compelling reason such as unacceptable side-effects, *or clear evidence that malaria is rare or unknown in your immediate area*. Advice from expatriates or nationals that pills are unnecessary, dangerous or useless should be treated with caution. So should pressure to change one type for another. An apparent absence of mosquitoes does not mean you cannot get malaria.

• Don't forget your tablets. Try to take them at the same time each day (or week), and keep them in the same place as part of a regular routine. A bottle of pills on the dining-room table, above the housekey rack, under your pillow or with your toothbrush are favourite memory-jogging sites. Always keep a supply with you when you are travelling, plus a few extra for forgetful friends. *Do not forget antimalarials when on holiday*.

• If you vomit within two hours of taking your antimalarial, repeat it once (Maloprim and mefloquine are exceptions and should not normally be repeated). If you have severe diarrhoea at the time of taking proguanil (Paludrine) repeat it once.

• Start antimalarials one week before travelling (or in the case of mefloquine ideally two weeks before). This ensures an adequate blood concentration of the drug and helps bring to light any unpleasant reactions to the drug when you still have time to change. Continue antimalarials for four weeks after you leave any malarious area.

Which antimalarials for which country?

Below are recommendations based on official information from the Malaria Reference Laboratory UK, 1995. Kindly read through the after-notes very carefully.

Country	Risk areas	Regimes 1st choice	2nd choice
Abu Dhabi	Very low risk	0	0
Afghanistan	Only below 2,000m May-November	C+P	**
Algeria	Very low risk	0	0
Angola	Whole country	MEF	C+P
Argentina	NW corner only	CHL	PRO
Azerbaijan	S border areas only	CHL	PRO
Bangladesh	All areas except east (Dhaka no risk)	C+P	**
	East, inc. Chittagong	MEF	C+P
Belize	Rural (no risk Belize Dist.)	CHL	PRO
Benin	Whole country	MEF	C+P
Bhutan	S districts only	C+P	**
Bolivia	Rural areas below 2,500m	C+P	MEF/MAL
Bolivia	Amazon Basin area	MEF	C+P
Botswana	N half only November-June	C+P	MEF/MAL
Brazil*	Amazon Basin, Mato Grosso, Maranhao, 'Legal Amazon'. Elsewhere low risk	MEF 0	C+P 0
Brunei	Very low risk	0	0
Burkina Faso	Whole country	MEF	C+P
Burundi	Whole country	MEF	C+P
Cambodia*	Western Provinces high risk	DOX	**
	Elsewhere (no risk in Phnom Penh)	MEF	**
Cameroon	Whole country	MEF	C+P
Cape Verde	Low risk	0	0

Central African Republic	Whole country	MEF	C+P
Chad	Whole country	MEF	C+P
China*	Main tourist areas low risk	0	0
	Hainan, Yunnan	MEF	**
	Other remote areas variable risk	CHL	**
Colombia	Most areas below 800m	MEF	C+P
Comoros	Whole country	MEF	C+P
Congo	Whole country	MEF	C+P
Costa Rica	Rural areas below 500m	CHL	PRO
Djibouti	Whole country	MEF	C+P
Dominican Republic	Generally low risk	CHL	PRO
Ecuador	Below 1,500m only	C+P	MEF/MAL
Egypt	Tourist areas very low risk	0	0
	El Fayoum June to October	CHL	PRO
El Salvador	Generally low risk	CHL	PRO
Equatorial Guinea	Whole country	MEF	C+P
Eritrea	Whole country	MEF	C+P
Ethiopia	Most of country. Addis central prob. safe	MEF	C+P
French Guiana	Whole country	MEF	C+P
Gabon	Whole country	MEF	C+P
Gambia	Whole country	MEF	C+P
Ghana	Whole country	MEF	C+P
Guatemala	Below 1,500m only	CHL	PRO
Guinea	Whole country	MEF	C+P
Guinea-Bissau	Whole country	MEF	C+P
Guyana	All interior regions	MEF	C+P
Haiti	Medium risk	CHL	PRO
Honduras	Medium risk but variable	CHL	PRO
Hong Kong	Very low risk	0	0
India*	Throughout, except above 2000m in north	C+P	**
Indonesia*	Bali and cities low risk	0	0
	Irian Jaya whole area	MEF	**
	Elsewhere variable	C+P	**
Iran	March-November only	C+P	**
Iraq	Rural north May-November	CHL	PRO
Ivory Coast	Whole country	MEF	C+P
Kenya	Whole country, central Nairobi prob. safe	MEF	C+P
Laos	Whole country except Vientiane (no risk)	MEF	**
Liberia	Whole country	MEF	C+P
Libya	Very low risk	0	0
Madagascar	Whole country	MEF	C+P
Malawi	Whole country	MEF	C+P
Malaysia*	Sabah	MEF	**
	Other deep-forested areas	C+P	**
	Other areas inc. cities Low risk	0	0
Mali	Whole country	MEF	C+P
Mauritania	South all year, north July-October	C+P	MEF/MAL
Mauritius	Rural areas only	CHL	**
Mexico*	Most tourist areas	0	0
	Some rural areas	CHL	PRO

Country	Area		
Morocco	Very low risk	0	0
Mozambique	Whole country	MEF	C+P
Myanmar (Burma)	Whole country	MEF	**
Namibia	Northern third November-June only	C+P	MEF/MAL
Nepal	Below 1,300m. No risk in	C+P	**
	Kathmandu valley	C+P	**
Nicaragua	Medium risk but variable	CHL	PRO
Niger	Whole country	MEF	C+P
Nigeria	Whole country	MEF	C+P
Oman	Medium risk whole country	C+P	**
Pakistan*	Below 2,000m	C+P	**
Panama	West of canal	CHL	PRO
	East of canal	C+P	MEF/MAL
Papua New Guinea	Below 1,800m	MEF	MAL+CHL
Paraguay	Rural areas October-May only	CHL	PRO
Peru	Rural below 1,500m	C+P	MEF/MAL
Philippines	Rural areas below 600m (no risk Cebu, Leyte, Bohol, Catanduanes)	C+P	**
Principe	Whole country	MEF	C+P
Rwanda	Whole country	MEF	C+P
Sao Tomé	Whole country	MEF	C+P
Saudi Arabia	Except N, E, central provs., Asir Plat. W border cities where low risk	C+P	**
Senegal	Whole country	MEF	C+P
Sierra Leone	Whole country	MEF	C+P
Singapore	No risk	0	0
Solomon Islands	Whole country	MEF	MAL+CHL
Somalia	Whole country	MEF	C+P
South Africa	Only NE, low alt. N&E Transvaal, E Natal down to 100km N of Durban	C+P	MEF/MAL
Sri Lanka	Except in and just south of Colombo	C+P	**
Sudan	Whole country	MEF	C+P
Surinam	Except Paramaribo and coast	MEF	C+P
Swaziland	Whole country	MEF	C+P
Syria	N border only May-October	CHL	PRO
Tajikistan	S border areas only	CHL	PRO
Tanzania	Whole country	MEF	C+P
Thailand*	Bangkok & main tourist centres low risk	0	0
	Rural areas	MEF	**
	Borders with Cambodia, Myanmar	DOX	**
Togo	Whole country	MEF	C+P
Tunisia	Very low risk	0	0
Turkey*	Most tourist areas very low risk	0	0
	Plain around Adona, Side, SE Anatolia, March-November only	CHL	PRO
Uganda	Whole country	MEF	C+P
Utd Arab Emirates	N rural areas only	C+P	**
Vanuatu	Whole country	MEF	MAL+CHL
Venezuela	Rural non-coastal areas (Caracas free)	C+P	MEF/MAL
	Amazon Basin area	MEF	C+P
Vietnam	Except cities, delta area	MEF	**

Yemen	Throughout country	C+P	**
Zaire	Whole country	MEF	C+P
Zambia	Whole country	MEF	C+P
Zimbabwe	Below 1,200m November-June	C+P	MEF/MAL
	Zambesi valley all year	MEF	**

Key to abbreviations used in list:

MEF	Take mefloquine 250mg one tablet weekly. Max. time 1 year
C+P	Take chloroquine 150mg (base) two tablets weekly *plus* proguanil 100mg (Paludrine) two tablets daily
CHL	Take chloroquine 150mg (base) two tablets weekly
PRO	Take proguanil 100mg (Paludrine) two tablets daily
DOX	Take doxycycline 100mg one tablet daily. Max. time 3 months
MEF/MAL	Take *either* mefloquine 250mg one tablet weekly *or* Maloprim one tablet weekly
MAL + CHL	Take Maloprim one tablet weekly *plus* chloroquine 150mg (base) two tablets weekly
0	No prophylaxis necessary. Report any fever
*	These countries have variable malarial risk. Obtain specific details after knowing your itinerary
**	No official 2nd choice. Ask for specific advice if unable to take 1st choice

Notes

1. *Pregnancy*. Chloroquine and proguanil are safe. Avoid mefloquine in first three months of pregnancy and avoid pregnancy within three months of stopping mefloquine. Although mefloquine is safe in the middle and latter thirds of pregnancy, it is not practical as it is not recommended when breastfeeding. Maloprim is safe in the middle and latter thirds of pregnancy but not in the first three months. Doxycycline should be avoided in pregnancy.

2. *Breastfeeding*. Chloroquine and proguanil are safe. Avoid Maloprim until at least six weeks after birth. Do not use doxycycline or mefloquine when breastfeeding.

3. Please see pages 74 for *dosages in children*. Mefloquine should not be used in children under 2 years old. Maloprim should not be used in children under six weeks old, and only after that age if a paediatric syrup is available (not available in UK). Doxycycline should not be used in children under 12. Chloroquine and proguanil are safe at all ages.

4. *Length of time in malarious areas*. Mefloquine is officially recommended for up to one year, though serious reported effects from longer-term use are rare. If you will be living in a country where mefloquine is recommended consider

changing to chloroquine and proguanil after one year or using this combination as an alternative from the beginning. Doxycycline is officially recommended for up to three months only, as experience with longer use is limited. Proguanil is safe indefinitely, as is chloroquine unless doses have in addition been used for treatment in which case an eye check should be carried out after five to six years of treatment and yearly thereafter (see also pages 151, 169).

5. *Formulation of chloroquine*: the normal adult dose is two 150mg (base) tablets. One tablet of chloroquine 150mg base is equivalent to one chloroquine sulphate 200mg tablet and to one chloroquine phosphate 250mg tablet. This means that the normal adult dose for prevention for all these chloroquine formulations is two tablets.

HOW DO YOU TREAT MALARIA?

If you think you may have malaria follow these steps:

1. See a reliable doctor or health worker and ask for a malaria smear. You should do this within eight hours of the start of fever or of other suspicious symptoms.

2. If the malaria smear is positive or the doctor believes you have malaria, make sure you receive treatment. If you are carrying your own standby tablets show them to the doctor.

3. If the smear is negative or the doctor says you have not got malaria self-treat anyway if *either* there is no obvious cause for your fever *or* your symptoms are not fully resolved within twenty-four hours with no recurrence.

4. If your symptoms continue or recur, whether or not you have treated for malaria or had a positive blood smear, make sure you get expert medical help as quickly as possible.

Although travellers off the beaten path should always carry standby treatment with them if in malarious areas, you are still recommended to see a doctor and get a blood smear, if possible.

Malaria suspected or confirmed must be appropriately treated without delay.

Recommended standby treatment for malaria

First choice for most areas (including all sub-Saharan Africa): **either** Fansidar alone, three tablets together **or** quinine 300mg, two tablets every eight hours for three days followed at the end of the three days by Fansidar three together. Fansidar resistance is increasing in Africa.

Special situations:

(a) Pregnancy and breastfeeding. Use quinine alone 300mg tablets, two every eight hours for three days. Avoid Fansidar. See a doctor.

(b) Areas definitely known to have no known chloroquine resistance (i.e. areas where first choice prophylaxis in country list is either CHL or 0). Take chloroquine 150mg (base) four together on days 1 and 2, two together on day 3. Total ten.

Please note: chloroquine is no longer recommended as a treatment for sub-Saharan Africa.

(c) Western Cambodia and border areas with Thailand and Myanmar (both sides of the frontier). Quinine 300mg tablets, two every eight hours for three days accompanied, not followed by, tetracycline 250mg four times daily for seven days.

(d) Use of mefloquine for treatment. Despite occasional troublesome side-effects this is generally a safe and effective treatment for all areas except (c) above for those not taking mefloquine as a prophylactic. The dose is mefloquine 250mg two together, followed by two together after twelve hours. Total four tablets (see page 78).

(e) Use of halofantrine (Halfan) for treatment. This should only be used as a standby if you have recently had an entirely normal ECG, and you do not suffer from any heart problems (see page 77).

MALARIA AND PREGNANCY

An attack of malaria, in particular malignant (P. falciparum) malaria can cause severe symptoms in pregnancy, including miscarriages and stillbirths. Ideally those who are pregnant should avoid areas where malignant malaria is common.

If this is not possible it is essential to take *prophylactics* without missing tablets, as well as full precautions to avoid mosquito bites (see pages 62–6). Pregnant women and children should avoid altogether travelling in western Cambodia or in the Thai border areas with Cambodia and Myanmar, as recommended treatment would not be safe for you.

Chloroquine and proguanil are entirely safe in pregnancy. Mefloquine and Maloprim are also considered to be safe except in the first three months of pregnancy. In addition pregnancy should be avoided within three months of discontinuing mefloquine. Doxycycline should be avoided in pregnancy. Take folic acid 5mg daily if you take proguanil or Maloprim.

For *treatment* quinine is safe and is the treatment of choice.

MALARIA AND BREASTFEEDING

Maloprim, Fansidar (or its equivalents) are harmful to newborn babies. They are also secreted in breast milk, and breastfeeding

Giving antimalarials to children is an acquired art

mothers should avoid both until at least six weeks after birth, using quinine for treatment instead.

Chloroquine, proguanil and quinine are safe during breast-feeding. Other antimalarial drugs, including mefloquine, should be avoided.

MALARIA AND CHILDREN

Babies and young children can quickly become seriously ill with malaria. Moreover their symptoms may not be typical so the diagnosis can easily be missed.

Ideally children under six months should avoid areas where malignant malaria is common. If this is not possible they should start antimalarials from birth (ideal) or from six weeks (essential) and sleep under a bed net impregnated with permethrin, or Icon. Babies under six weeks, if travelling in an area where Maloprim is recommended, should instead take proguanil (Paludrine) and chloroquine (see Tables below). Under the age of 2 they should only take Maloprim if a syrup is available.

Table 1 Prophylactic dosages for children (i.e. for prevention)
(as fractions of the adult dose)

Age	Chloroquine Paludrine	Maloprim	Mefloquine
0–5 weeks	1/8	Not recommended	Not recommended
6 weeks to 1 year	1/4	1/8	Not recommended
1–5 years (10–19kg)	1/2	1/4	Not used in the under-2s or below 15kg; 2–5 years, 1/4
6–11 years (20–39kg)	3/4	1/2	1/2 (6–8 years); 3/4 (9–11 years and up to 45kg)
12 years plus (up to 40kg)	Adult dose	Adult dose	Adult dose

Doxycycline should be avoided in those under the age of 12.

Table 2 Treatment dosages for children are as follows:

	Fansidar or Metakelfin:
Two months to 4 years	1/2 tablet (i.e. 1/6th adult dose)
4–6 years	1 tablet
7–9 years	1 1/2 tablets
10–14 years	2 tablets
Over 15 years	3 tablets

Quinine: 10mg/kg every eight hours for seven days.

Chloroquine is available in the UK as a syrup (Nivaquine syrup). Some children prefer this to a crushed tablet, others are deeply suspicious. Maloprim (Deltaprim) is available as a syrup in Zimbabwe and some surrounding countries.

Other antimalarial drugs are only available as tablets. They should be crushed and given on a spoon with jam, honey or something sweet. Alternatively they can be dissolved with sugar in a little milk, or rolled in butter, peanut butter or a favourite salty savoury and placed near the back of the tongue. As a *last resort* a tablet can be crushed, added to sugary milk, drawn up in a clean syringe from which the needle has been removed and introduced slowly down the side of the tongue. Giving antimalarials to children is an acquired art.

NOTE: The dosages in Tables 1 and 2 follow the recommendation of the UK Malaria Reference Laboratory. It differs in some details from advice on the instruction slips which accompany some bottles of antimalarial tablets and also from World Health Organisation sources. This is because there is not yet international agreement.

MALARIA AFTER RETURNING HOME

'Flu' may be malaria. Make sure you report any suspicious symptoms without delay, especially in children. You should either report to a GP or go direct to the accident and emergency department of a main hospital, explain you have come from a malarious area and insist you have a blood smear. If this is negative and the fever persists or worsens you should have a repeat test carried out, preferably at a tropical diseases centre. It is *not* safe simply to take chloroquine and hope for the best. If you take your standby of Fansidar or quinine you must seek advice if you are not improving within twenty-four hours.

Note that if you are in or near London you can go to the Hospital for Tropical Diseases at any time of the day or night without a letter, if you think you may have malaria (see page 211 for this and other centres).

If you have had recurrent attacks of malaria and are now home for good or for a long leave, it is sensible to take a course of primaquine to eradicate the persistent forms of benign malaria which may otherwise plague you for months. You should discuss this at your tropical health check.

If you have been brought up in a malarious country, then come to study or live in the UK for more than twelve months you may lose your immunity. This means you are at risk of getting malaria on return to a malarious area. It is worth taking prophylactics for six months after returning and being very careful then, and subsequently, to report and treat any symptoms which could be malaria.

NOTES ON COMMONLY USED DRUGS

When in the tropics, probably sooner rather than later, the conversation will turn to malaria. Details of the latest therapeutic fashion mingled with advice, good, bad and indifferent will soon fill the air. It is helpful to know basic information both about the medicines you may be using as well as those others are talking about. A large number of different trade names add further to the confusion. Here is a simple field guide.

Amodiaquine (Camoquin, Flavoquine, Florquine, Miaquine)

Uses: Was used for prophylaxis, now discontinued owing to risk of blood disorders. Occasionally still used for treatment in chloroquine-sensitive areas.

Chloroquine (Aralen, Avloclor, Chinamine, Delagil, Imagon, Malariquine, Malarivon, Nivaquine, Plaquenol, Resochin, Sanioquin, Tresochin)

Uses: For prevention and treatment as described in text.

Warnings: nausea, itching – and rashes especially in Africans. May make psoriasis worse. It should not be used in those with a history of epilepsy. Chloroquine is safe in pregnancy and during lactation. It is best to take it with food.

It is available from chemists without a prescription and from travel clinics.

Eyes and chloroquine: damage to the retina is not now thought by most experts to occur if weekly chloroquine *only* is taken. If however chloroquine is in addition used for treatment it may accumulate in the retina in which case regular eye checks should be carried out. Some experts still advise checks if regular chloroquine at a dose of 300mg (base) per week has been taken continuously for six years or more (see also page 169).

Chlorproguanil (Lapudrine). An alternative to proguanil (probably slightly less effective) taken as 20mg tablet twice weekly, or better, daily.

Warnings: as for proguanil.

Doxycycline (Vibramycin, Nordox)

Uses: as a prophylactic at a dose of one (100mg) tablet per day for Cambodia (especially western) and Thai/Cambodia, Thai/Myanmar border areas. It is an alternative for other malarious regions.

Warnings: should not be used in children 12 or under nor in pregnancy and breastfeeding. It can increase the risk of vaginal thrush, diarrhoea and sunburn, and if taking it you should avoid the sun or take extra protective measures. Take it with plenty of fluids and not just before lying down. Experience of side-effects for periods of longer than three months is limited.

Fansidar (The trade name for sulfadoxine 500mg plus pyrimethamine 25mg)

Uses: for treatment of malaria as described in text. Should not be used for prophylaxis.

Warnings: generally safe if used for treatment. Should be avoided in those sensitive to sulphonamides or pyrimethamine, in pregnancy and during the first six weeks of lactation. Should not be used in children under two months. Sometimes causes skin rashes and allergic reactions.

Available on prescription and from some travel clinics.

Halofantrine (Halfan)

Uses: *should only be used under medical supervision*. It is an effective treatment against most forms of malaria, including chloroquine-resistant strains but the course of six tablets should be repeated after one week to prevent recurrences.

As Halfan syrup it is an effective treatment for children but it is not available in the United Kingdom.

Warnings: cases of serious cardiac effects, including deaths, have occasionally been reported. Halfan should only be used in travellers who have had a recent, normal ECG, and avoided if there is any history of heart disease. It must be taken on an empty stomach. Avoid during pregnancy and delay conception for at least one month after completing a course of treatment.

It is not safe during lactation.

It should not be used for treatment unless no other medication is available.

Available on prescription only.

Maloprim (The trade name for pyrimethamine 12.5mg plus dapsone 100mg) (Deltaprim, Malasone)

Uses: for prophylaxis as in text: available on prescription.

Warnings: unlikely to cause blood disorders if taken at normal dose of one per week. Avoid in liver or kidney disease, first three months of pregnancy and first six weeks of lactation. Those sensitive to sulphonamides sometimes develop an allergic reaction and should take it for a trial period of two weeks before deciding to use it long term. Those who are pregnant must take folic acid in addition.

Mefloquine (Lariam, Mephaquin)

Uses: for prophylaxis as in text. It gives better protection than any other drug in areas of chloroquine resistance. It can be used as a treatment if no other effective drug is available under medical supervision, and providing it has not been used as a prophylactic. The dose for treatment is 250mg, two tablets together, then two further tablets after twelve hours. (Mephaquin comes as 228mg tablets in USA.)

Warnings: is generally safe and fairly well tolerated when used as a prophylactic drug but avoid if history of psychiatric illness, liver or cardiac disorder. May occasionally cause nausea, dizziness, fine tremor, loss of fine co-ordination, vivid dreams or psychological disorders, especially anxiety, irritability, depression or hallucinations. Side-effects usually become apparent in the first two or three weeks. Not to be used in first three months of pregnancy (delay conception till three months after using), nor in lactation. Should not be taken by those being treated with beta-blocking drugs. It should be avoided in those with a personal or a family history of epilepsy. The side-effects when used for treatment can be more severe.

Available on prescription and from some travel clinics.

Mefloquine should carry a social health warning: avoid excessive discussion of real or imagined side-effects.

Primaquine (Neo-quipenyl)

Uses: prescribed by doctors to eradicate recurring attacks of benign malaria; usual dosage is 15mg daily for fourteen days, but this sometimes needs to be doubled.

Warnings: in those who lack an enzyme known as G6PD, it may cause a serious reaction and a G6PD blood test should be performed before treatment, ideally on everyone, and essentially on those of African, Asian or Mediterranean descent. May also cause rashes and other allergic reactions. Should be avoided in pregnancy.

Proguanil 100mg (Paludrine, Chlorguanide, Lepadina, Palusil, Proguanide, Tirian)

Uses: for prevention of malaria as described in text.

Warnings: frequently causes mouth ulcers (continue if possible) and occasionally hair loss (in which case stop taking it). May also cause nausea and stomach discomfort, so should be taken with food, preferably in the evening. Safe in pregnancy and lactation. Can affect the dose of anticoagulants.

Available from chemists without prescription and from travel clinics. Proguanil is little used by those from North America.

Pyrimethamine (Daraprim, Chloridin, Malocide, Tindurin, Syraprim)

Uses: this was widely used for prevention of malaria but is no longer recommended.

Quinine (Quinimax, Quinoforme)

Uses: for treatment of all forms of malaria as described in text.

Warnings: may cause headache, tinnitus, dizziness, nausea and allergic reactions. Can be used in pregnancy and lactation if chloroquine is ineffective. Should ideally be used under medical supervision, especially if mefloquine has been used as a prophylactic. Quinine is generally considered a safe drug.

Available on prescription and from some travel clinics.

Other drugs and combinations sometimes used:

Daraclor is pyrimethamine and chloroquine.

Fansimef is sulfadoxine, pyrimethamine and mefloquine and is used for treatment under medical supervision as an alternative to Fansidar.

Lapoquin is chlorproguanil plus chloroquine.

Metakelfin is sulfalene and pyrimethamine and is used as an alternative to Fansidar.

Tetracycline (Achromycin, Cyclomycin, Panmycin, Tetracyn etc) is occasionally used for treatment in areas where there is chloroquine and Fansidar resistance. In these cases a course of quinine is followed or accompanied by tetracycline 250mg four times daily for seven days. It should not be used in those sensitive to tetracyclines, in pregnancy and in children under 12.

SUMMARY

Malaria is a serious nuisance at best and a fatal illness at worst. If going to a malarious area take your tablets without missing them and sleep under a bed net impregnated with permethrin. Keep covered or carefully protected with insect repellent when you go out in the evening. Make sure you get prompt treatment for any fever or serious illness both while abroad or if symptoms develop after returning home.

AVOIDING AIDS

WHAT YOU NEED TO KNOW

The difference between AIDS and HIV

AIDS stands for the Acquired Immune Deficiency Syndrome. It is caused by the Human Immunodeficiency Virus (HIV) which attacks the immune system. Usually within three months of being infected with the virus, antibodies develop to HIV and the blood antibody test becomes HIV positive.

Infection with HIV usually leads to AIDS though the length of time between becoming infected and developing AIDS is extremely variable, averaging about ten years. During this 'latent period' the person infected with HIV is largely free of symptoms but is infectious to others. Once AIDS has developed death usually occurs within two years.

The extent of the problem

Worldwide at the time of writing – early 1995 – there are more than one million reported cases of AIDS, but several times that number are thought to exist. The number of those infected with HIV is now estimated at about fifteen million. In a few countries up to 25% of the adult urban population is HIV positive.

More than 160 countries have now reported AIDS and the number of cases from Asia and parts of Latin America, as well as from Africa, is increasing rapidly.

How AIDS is spread

• Through *having sex* with an infected partner. Worldwide this is the main method of spread.

• Through receiving *infected blood transfusions* or blood-derived products.

• Through *dirty needles*, syringes, lancets, scalpels and dental instruments.

• Occasionally through *surface* spread where infected blood and other body fluids are in contact with mucous membranes and injured skin (cuts, abrasions, chapping).

● *Razorblades*, shared toothbrushes, and instruments used for ear-piercing and tattooing, may cause occasional cases.

● Through spread from *mother to child* at or during birth.

● HIV infection is occasionally spread from mother to child through infected *breast milk*.

HIV infection is *not spread* through normal social contact even if close and prolonged. There is no evidence that insects, including mosquitoes or bed-bugs, can spread AIDS, nor do toilet seats, swimming pools, cutlery or shared communion cups.

By living in a country where AIDS is common you face a *potentially* greater risk of becoming infected than you would in your home country. *But* by following a few commonsense rules your risk of infection can become negligible.

WHAT YOU NEED TO DO

These precautions will minimise your risk:

Before you go:

● Complete *immunisations*.

● Have a *dental* check.

● Find out your *blood group* and keep a record with you.

● Take a supply of recommended *antimalarial* tablets and other recommended antimalarial equipment if going to a malarious area.

● Take a *needle and syringe* kit.

● Consider taking an AIDS *protection kit* containing an intravenous giving set and bottles of plasma substitute.

● Plan ahead if *pregnancy* is possible.

● *Decide to abstain* from casual sexual encounters.

● *Take condoms* with you unless you consider your principles, beliefs and defence mechanisms will *guarantee your safe behaviour even at times of stress or loneliness*.

● Resolve *not to get drunk* as many cases of HIV are contracted in an alcoholic haze.

While abroad:

● *Avoid casual sexual encounters.*

The only way of being certain to avoid sexually transmitted HIV infection is to be permanently loyal to one partner who is known to be HIV negative. In practice this means that only if you abstain from pre-and extramarital sex can you be certain to avoid infection. Remember that safe sex only means safer sex. *Although condoms theoretically give high protection, the effects of carelessness, splitting and slippage make them far less than 100% safe, especially if you have been drinking.*

As many as 75% of sex workers in some cities of the world are HIV positive.

Women as far as possible should avoid situations, lifestyles and inappropriate clothing which might increase their risk of being raped, or misinterpreted.

● *Avoid road accidents.*

These are a major risk because serious accidents often necessitate medical treatment and blood transfusions. Please read the section on page 85.

● *Avoid blood transfusions from unknown or untested sources (see pages 86–9).*

In case of an accident or emergency where serious blood loss is occurring you or your companion should follow the guidelines on page 87.

● *Avoid dirty needles and syringes.*

Produce your own needles and syringes except in health facilities where you reliably know that sterile, sealed, disposable needles and syringes are always used. Try to ascertain that the nurse actually does use the needle and syringe you provide. This will require tact and courtesy!

● *In addition:*

Produce your own lancet for a malaria smear.

Wherever possible *use medicines* that can be taken by mouth rather than by injection. You may need to be assertive.

Avoid locally made gammaglobulin or other blood- or serum-derived products.

Take full precautions to avoid malaria, as severe malaria increases the need for treatment by injection or blood transfusion.

Plan any non-urgent surgery or dentistry for when you come home.

Health care workers will need more detailed advice. It is important they discuss through the full implications of working in an area where the risk of HIV cannot be entirely eliminated.

On return home:

You may start to worry that you have become infected with HIV. Unless you have been *knowingly* at risk the chance of becoming infected is extremely remote.

Anyone who wishes to have an HIV test is entitled to do so, either through their GP, or as part of their 'Tropical Health Check' or at a hospital STD clinic. Confidentiality is ensured.

To be largely sure of any possible infection showing on the blood test it is worth delaying any final test until at least ninety days after any last possible exposure.

Provided the test is negative and you can record an occupational reason or specific non-recurring risk while abroad, you are extremely unlikely to be declined by an insurance company or charged a higher premium. If you are you can appeal. A statement of practice is available from the Association of British Insurers, 51 Gresham Street, London EC2V 7HQ.

Entry certificates

A few countries require certificates stating that you have tested HIV negative. A negative test carried out not more than ninety days before entry and accompanied by a doctor's signed and stamped certificate stating this was carried out in a WHO-accredited lab., is usually sufficient, though some countries will expect you to have a test after arrival if you are planning to reside in that country. Check with the embassy of the country in question if in doubt, or with a specialist travel clinic.

SUMMARY

AIDS in adults is a preventable disease. *It is better to be entirely safe than for ever sorry*.

PREVENTING ROAD AND SWIMMING ACCIDENTS

In many surveys *road accidents* are the commonest cause of expatriate death and head the list for emergency repatriations. On top of this they increase the risk of AIDS because of emergency surgery, injections and blood transfusions.

The majority of road accidents can be prevented:

● Fit and wear *seat belts* to both front and rear seats, and ensure that these are used by all, including children. *Wearing seat belts is probably the single most important health precaution you can take when overseas (or at home).*

● *Keep your vehicle in good condition* by regular servicing and make sure tyres are adequate, and brakes and lights are working properly.

● Try to *avoid driving when tired*, or for prolonged periods, or overnight or without a co-driver. Never drink and drive, or drive when taking medicines which make you drowsy.

● *Leave plenty of time* for journeys so you are not in a hurry.

● *Choose drivers, taxis and rickshaws with care*, and, as far as your ingenuity allows, make sure that lights, tyres and brakes are in good order before setting out. Ensure your driver is alert and not under the influence of drugs or alcohol. 'Close-face bargaining' can enable you to observe pupils, and smell breath.

● *Ride* in the safest part of the vehicle.

● Motor cyclists should wear *crash helmets* (or change to a safer form of transport).

● When *crossing the road* remember the direction of traffic flow. Take special care of children if visiting a city after living in a rural area.

For the *procedure* to follow in a serious road accident see page 89.

Swimming accidents are common overseas both in the sea and swimming pool and medical support to save life – and disability – that much harder to obtain.

Prevent *sea accidents* by:

● only swimming in areas known to be free from dangerous currents, sharks, poisonous fish (e.g. stone fish, sting rays) and jellyfish (e.g. box jellyfish);

● never going out of your depth;

● always swimming with a companion;

● never swimming if you have been drinking alcohol;

● avoiding sunburn;

● avoiding polluted areas and not taking in water through your mouth.

Prevent *accidents in swimming pools* by:

● never running along the edge of the pool;

● never drinking alcohol before or during swimming;

● never diving without first having carefully checked the depth of the water;

● never diving into a cloudy pool;

● avoiding polluted pools;

● avoiding sunburn;

• keeping a careful eye on your children.

Finally, after your swim or at any other time be careful on your *hotel balcony*. Several travellers die each year because of a low or weak balcony – or a high blood alcohol level.

KNOWING ABOUT BLOOD TRANSFUSIONS

OCCASIONS WHEN YOU MIGHT NEED BLOOD

The commonest reason for needing a blood transfusion when overseas is because of a road accident. Other causes include: bleeding during an operation, blood loss before, during or after childbirth, severe malaria and a bleeding peptic ulcer. You can minimise these risks by commonsense precautions, a healthy lifestyle and planning ahead.

Serious blood loss – of more than 25% of the blood volume – means you will require emergency transfusion. However for all but the most urgent situations you can start treatment using a plasma substitute to replace fluid lost until such time as you can reach a safe donor or obtain supplies of safe blood.

MAKING SURE BLOOD IS SAFE

Blood in order to be safe must fulfil two criteria: freedom from infection and belonging to a compatible group.

It should be free from infection

This includes HIV, hepatitis B and C, syphilis and malaria. When you go to a UK Blood Donor Clinic, tests are carried out on all the above except malaria, at which time your blood group is also ascertained. However when you simply have a blood group arranged in a GP surgery, hospital lab. or travel clinic, tests for infection are not necessarily carried out. Blood supplies in developing countries are often inadequately tested or not tested at all.

There are three ways to reduce the risk of receiving HIV-infected blood when overseas:

• Only accept blood which has been HIV-tested immediately before you receive it.

• Only receive blood from a donor whose lifestyle you trust. This is important because blood infected with HIV may still test negative for a period of three months after becoming infected, and during this 'window' period can still pass on HIV disease.

• Use a plasma substitute until you can reach a source of known safe blood (see below).

Blood should belong to a compatible group (see Table 3 on page 90)

Even when compatible blood groups are used, blood should still be cross-matched to further reduce the risk of serious reaction. In this test drops of blood from the person giving and the person receiving blood are mixed together. Cross-matching should ideally be done just before the transfusion is set up.

REMEMBER: blood from an unknown source should be avoided except in life-threatening emergencies.

PRACTICAL STEPS YOU SHOULD TAKE

1. Know your blood group before going abroad

Make sure that you and all family members, or others in a group for whom you are responsible, know their blood groups. Each person should keep a written record of their blood group with them at all times. Similarly parents should keep a note of all family members, and group leaders of all in their group.

Blood grouping can either be arranged through your GP or local hospital; both will usually charge. Alternatively you can become a blood donor and have it checked free of charge (see page 18).

2. Join a trusted donor group overseas

On arrival at your destination obtain a list of local, trusted donors, and consider adding your name. Most companies or projects employing expatriate staff will have such a list (sometimes known as a Walking Blood Bank) as will British embassies. If they don't you can set one up yourself.

You may not know, or trust, all names on this list. *This means that you should make a point of identifying two or three easily accessible expatriates with a compatible group whose blood you would be happy to receive.* Make a note of who they are and their emergency contact addresses.

3. Consider taking an AIDS and hepatitis B protection kit

This should at least contain an intravenous giving set and two or more bottles of plasma substitute. Consider taking it if you expect to do much travel in areas where AIDS is common. At the time of an accident its use does depend on someone being present who knows how to set it up, though simple instructions are usually included. If you do take one abroad make sure you always have it with you on road journeys. It is no use having it under your bed if you've just had a road accident 100 kilometres from home, but also remember not to let it overheat in the hot boot of a car.

4. Know a transfusion procedure in case of an accident

This will include:

● *Giving/receiving* first aid, and prevention of further bleeding where possible. (See page 230 for details of *First Aid Manual*.)

● *Setting up* an intravenous line and running in plasma substitute if kit and health worker are available and if the injured person shows signs of shock (much blood loss – often concealed – with fast pulse, cold extremities, low blood pressure).

● *Admission* to a reliable health facility.

● *Arrangement for blood transfusion* if needed, as soon as available, and from a trusted donor or safe source. Blood from an untested or unsafe source should be refused unless in a life-threatening emergency.

COMPATIBLE BLOOD GROUPS

Everyone belongs to group O, A, B, or AB. In addition everyone is Rhesus (D) positive or negative. Blood has to be compatible for both the group and the Rhesus sign, otherwise serious reactions can occur with transfusions. It is ideal to receive blood from someone with an identical blood group to your own, or who is O Rhesus negative (universal donor). However blood can also be given and received according to Table 3:

Table 3 Compatible Blood Groups

Blood group	Can give to	Can receive from
O+	O+, A+, B+, AB+	O+, O−
O−	All groups	O−
A+	A+, AB+	A+, A−, O+, O−
A−	A+, A−, AB+, AB−	A−, O−
B+	B+, AB+	B+, B−, O+, O−
B−	B+, B−, AB+, AB−	B−, O−
AB+	AB+	All groups
AB−	AB−, AB+	AB−, A−, B−, O−

COPING WITH STRESS
by Dr Ruth Fowke

STRESS OR STIMULUS?

It sometimes seems that most people are either suffering from stress themselves or setting up seminars to help those who are. Stress is indeed an ever-present part of modern living and few people will find that jumping on a plane for an overseas assignment will automatically lead them to a stress-free nirvana. Indeed for many working abroad, levels of stress are high. This means that learning to recognise, prevent and deal with stress is one of the most useful lessons we can learn, both before and during our time overseas.

It is important to understand that a situation which is of little consequence to one person may be highly stressful to someone else, and for a third may be the very stimulus which leads to appropriate action. One answer to stress therefore is to 'Know yourself' – and to learn what situations are stressful to you.

Stimulation is necessary for effective living. No stimulation generally means no achievement. The point in time or intensity when stimulation turns to stress is an individual matter. This means it is helpful for each individual and family to find out the optimum level of stimulation for their own wellbeing. In this way they are likely 'to have a good work-out rather than to rust out or burn out':

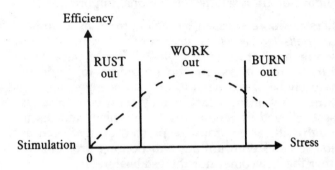

SPECIFIC OVERSEAS STRESSES

Living together with other expatriates can often be the biggest stress factor of all. Remember that what stresses one person or family may merely amuse or stimulate another. These individual differences to stress can in themselves cause tension especially in those living and working in confined circumstances without the possibility of relief from one another's company. Just realising this fact can in itself help the situation. Some can only recharge their personal batteries with plenty of people around them to join in the activity, others crave to be alone for a while. A routine lifestyle is essential for some, while a random one is necessary for the health of others. Some people work best in sequential, even steps, while others can only do so in bursts of energy with pauses between. The output of both may be similar but the method of working is so different that each can mistrust and come to dislike the other. It is difficult for larks and owls to agree on the best time to start work. But even if they can't agree they can at least learn to accept that each has a different metabolism (and that God created them both).

Loneliness is a further cause of stress to many. It will strike people in various ways and at different times and is particularly hard to manage when the partner, friend or rest of the group seems to be adapting well. The operative words here are 'seem to' because gentle discussion often reveals that others too are having or have had the same symptoms. Just knowing that others feel the same brings considerable relief. It is helpful also to preplan activities, ideally with others, during any festivals, birthdays or anniversaries of personal importance.

Others are more stressed by feeling themselves to have *inadequate skills for the job assigned*, or having no clear role, job description or areas of responsibility (see page 116). Some are threatened by having no precedent to guide them, or conversely being expected to follow uncongenial or rigid procedures. Any of these factors may contribute to stress which is best relieved by identifying the problem and discussing it through with an appropriate person, even if such a person needs some careful hunting out. Bottling problems up helps neither the newcomer nor the establishment.

For those working overseas there are further particular pressures that may push them towards the slippery slope. They generally have to do with living and working in an environment where:

● *attitudes* are different, especially professional ones. You may be working to different standards and a different timescale in a place with different ethics and values. Recognise these things and talk them through with someone.

● *privacy and autonomy* may be markedly reduced. To be the subject of continual scrutiny wherever you go, and yet not be free to go where you choose, can be very stressful. There are often small ways you can increase your range once you have recognised the problem.

● *your role is very different*. It may be unclear, unfamiliar and perhaps uncongenial. To go from being an established leader to finding yourself an insignificant newcomer can be hard, especially if the skills you are bringing do not seem to be wanted or valued. Acknowledging this may help to take the sting out of it.

● *your sense of identity may be shaken*. If you stay long enough to be at home in the culture you may not feel you belong to either the new or your previous one. Bilingual children may be more at home in their host country than the 'home' one, which can be a real stress for their parents. Talk it out with someone, don't bottle it up.

● *Violence*, police surveillance and political uncertainty are commonplace. To be living always in a state of maximum alertness is very hard on the nerves. Make sure you take all the 'R and R' you are entitled to.

SIGNS OF STRESS

As stimulus turns to stress work output gradually lowers, generally accompanied by a compulsion to keep working. Guidelines for healthy living, especially those regarding recreation and leisure time, are ignored 'just for once' or 'until I catch up'. Often however the person never does make up lost ground and a vicious circle develops.

Healthy and unhealthy life patterns can be represented by the two triangles, in this diagram:

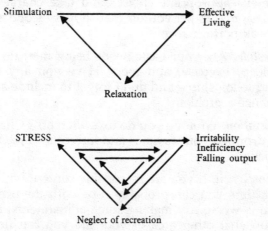

A person who slides into the second type of lifestyle continues to work harder and put in longer hours with less overall effect. Those who continue in this way are likely to lose concentration, have memory lapses and seem 'less alive'. They may become irritable and humourless, even anxious and depressed. They become more rigid in thought and behaviour, have a narrowed focus and seem to lose their normal elasticity and the ability to recover when pulled apart. All these things may be more easily detected by their friends than by themselves. More than this, their whole immune system may be weakened so that their resistance to infection is lowered.

If at this stage no break is taken a return to normal can only be achieved by total removal from the situation and a period of lengthy recovery. Fortunately you can avoid a decline into burn-out or breakdown by taking time away from work and the demands of others, and by absorbing yourself in some quite different activity.

LIFESTYLE REVIEW

Learn to recognise when your personal efficiency curve begins to decline, and give your lifestyle a shake-out to prevent burn-out.

The aim of doing this is to help you generate options so that you can make appropriate choices and take charge of your life. It is designed to get you off that slippery slope and back towards peak performance:

- *Your lifestyle.* Are your basic needs being met, do you get enough sleep, exercise, and food? Have you any time for friends and fellowship – and don't forget to include some fun too. Is finance a problem?

- *Your relaxation.* What do you do to 'switch off'? Chances are you have dropped your hobbies and interests – take them up again, quickly!

- *Work satisfaction.* If you are reasonably content with 70% of your work time you can probably cope with the other 30%. If the ratio is worse, try making some adjustments, and also consider in what other area of your life you can find some fulfilment.

- *Relationships:* are they kept in good repair? You may need to give more time and attention to some of them.

- *Your expectations* of yourself, and of others. Perhaps you need to go for that which is 'good enough', rather than perfect.

- *Areas of uncertainty.* Check out any information that seems ambiguous or unclear. Make clear statements and requests yourself. Tell the relevant people that you are stressed – don't assume that they know; tell them plainly.

STRESS STRATEGIES

Just as one person's stress can be another person's stimulus so patterns of relaxation differ greatly between different types of people. What one person finds relaxing may seem boring – or incomprehensible – to someone else. The answer is to discover your own coping strategies, and find out what forms of relaxation will be both effective and possible in your overseas location. Some will have to train themselves to become detached from the 'Protestant Work Ethic'. Others won't find this difficult at all once they 'have permission', or can quote doctor's advice.

Here are some further practical suggestions:

● *Avoid* self-medication with 'leisure' drugs, tranquillisers, nicotine or too much alcohol, coffee, and caffeine-containing drinks.

● *Do* get enough sleep, change of occupation and exercise.

● *Do* talk your situation and feelings through with someone.

● *Do* develop an absorbing hobby or interest outside your work.

● *Don't:* (a) carry on working if you get sick – better to rest up before you get really laid up; (b) put off taking time off; (c) neglect your friendships; (d) forget to laugh – it's a good way of defusing stress; (e) forget to take exercise – that regular walk, hour in the pool, or game of volleyball can help to unjangle your nerves.

AND FINALLY . . .

Someone has worked out that we ourselves can help to solve 50% of our problems, another 30% can be eased if we have the courage to ask for help, and only 20% will remain despite what we do. Although we can't alter this 20% we can change our own attitude by a combination of acceptance, prayer or spiritual discipline. When our attitude alters our stress diminishes – especially if we take appropriate steps to deal with the 80% we can do something about.

Most important of all is to keep a sense of proportion, to nurture a sense of humour, to avoid fatigue and to remember to switch off regularly by switching on to some form of recreation and relaxation. Even taking time to slow down, to do some deep breathing, and to stretch, then relax every muscle group from toe to head is beneficial as are more formal relaxation tapes which are helpful to some.

Anyone who has never been stressed has probably never lived life to the full. Only by living to our particular limits do we know what these limits are, but wise and healthy people, having discovered these, do not often, or for long, *push themselves or allow others to push them beyond their threshold*. Learning to say No (in an appropriate way) to whatever requests put you over your own personal stress level is the best way of coping with it.

Finally, with the subject of stress so topical in our culture, we need to make sure we do not get stressed about being stressed, or worry we are about to have a nervous breakdown. Some gentle humour, self-detachment and remembrance of friends who have been able to tough it out when circumstances demanded it, can help us to keep things in perspective, and tide us over difficult times.

If despite all this you ever feel that stress is really getting the better of you do let someone know. It is much quicker to put things right at this stage than to let them drag on. Consider having a personal debrief on returning home (see page 148) and remember it is no disgrace to be 'honourably wounded' when you are serving abroad, or at home, and wounds do heal.

PHYSICAL HAZARDS

ALTITUDE

Many travellers can't resist the temptation of climbing a near (or distant) mountain peak, or fitting in a high-altitude trek while the opportunity is there. Although the rewards are great so are the potential risks especially if your time available is short, your preparation and equipment limited, or you don't want to appear a wimp by failing to keep up with your companions.

Mountains carry several health hazards. The risk of *accidents* is greater, most of which can be prevented by careful preparation, common sense and not being in an undue hurry. The risks of exposure to *sun*, *wind*, and *cold* are also greater (see pages 100–4).

ACUTE MOUNTAIN SICKNESS (AMS, ALTITUDE SICKNESS)

A common condition in mountains is *acute mountain sickness* (AMS). This does not just affect the elderly and unfit. Indeed the young volunteer, able to climb fast and hoping to do a quick ascent before returning to the UK, or before the weather turns, is at the greatest risk.

AMS in its milder forms affects about 50% of unacclimatised travellers at 3,500 metres (about 11,000 feet) and 80–90% at 5,000 metres (about 15,500 feet). The danger of AMS is that it can progress quickly and unpredictably to life-threatening cerebral and pulmonary oedema.

As a general rule watch out for AMS in any journey to above about 3,500 metres (about 11,000 feet), especially if you have not acclimatised for a day or two at an intermediate altitude. Symptoms may be delayed and not become apparent for twenty-four to forty-eight hours. A minority of people are affected from about 2,000 metres (6,500 feet) upwards.

If you are planning to trek or climb above 3,500 metres familiarise yourself with the symptoms in Table 4.

Prevention of AMS

● Before travelling to heights above 3,500 metres stay for one or two days at that height or just below. *Then make a slow ascent*.

● Above 3,500 metres spend each *night* not more than 300 metres (about 1,000 feet) above the last. One full rest day should be allowed every two or three days or every 1,000 metres (about 3,000 feet). Where overnight shelters do not allow this, take extra care. Mt Kilimanjaro (5,895 metres, 19,340 feet) is a case in point where shelters are at about 9,000, 12,000 and 14,500 feet. (For the sake of simplicity feet/metre conversions are approximate.)

● Try to follow the maxim 'climb high, but sleep lower'. Symptoms often come on at night and can be masked by tiredness and exhaustion and not be noticed by your companions.

● Avoid if possible taking sleeping tablets at high altitude (they depress breathing).

● Drink extra fluids.

● Consider taking Diamox (acetazolamide) 500mg sustained-release tablets one at night for three nights before ascent and until reaching 5,000 metres. An alternative is nifedipine (Adalat) 20mg three times daily. These need to be prescribed by a doctor.

Treatment of AMS

● If signs of benign AMS develop remain at the same altitude for forty-eight hours.

● If symptoms of pulmonary or cerebral oedema develop, *descend to a lower altitude as quickly as possible*. Whether by staggering at the side of a companion or being carried on an improvised stretcher descend to an altitude where symptoms largely disappear.

● Although Diamox and nifedipine may help to both prevent

and treat AMS, it is far better to rely on slow ascents to prevent AMS and quick descents to treat it. Portable hyperbaric chambers, 'the Gamow Bag', have proved their worth in mountaineering when quick descent is not possible. Oxygen where available can also be life saving.

It is reasonable for healthy people up to the age of 65–70 to fly into altitudes of 3,500 metres, but symptoms of AMS are likely to occur.

Table 4 **Acute Mountain Sickness**

Benign form	*Severe form* *High altitude cerebral oedema*
Headache	Pounding headache unrelieved by painkillers
Loss of appetite/nausea	Drowsiness and confusion leading to coma
Dizziness	Unsteady, staggering walk
Disturbed sleep	Double vision
	High altitude pulmonary oedema
Breathlessness on mild exertion	Breathlessness at rest
Irregular 'sighing' breathing	Cough with or without sputum, possibly bloodstained
	Blue lips
ACTION:	ACTION:
Stay at same (or lower) altitude for 48 hours	Descend without delay to lower altitude until symptoms become
Descend if symptoms worsen	substantially improved

For those over about 70 or with known heart or lung problems: any pre-existing symptoms such as shortness of breath, or swollen ankles are likely to get worse with altitude, especially in those on betablocking drugs. The treatment is to go back down the hill, and only go to heights above 2,000 metres (about 6,500 feet) in the first place if your doctor gives you clearance, after detailed assessment.

Table 5 **Heights above sea level of some high-altitude cities**

	Height above sea level
	Metres
Lhasa, Tibet	3,900
La Paz, Bolivia	3,800
Quito, Ecuador	3,000
Toluca, Mexico	2,900
Cuzco, Peru	2,800
Cochabamba, Bolivia	2,800
Bogota, Colombia	2,800
Addis Ababa, Ethiopia	2,600
Arequipa, Peru	2,500
Mexico City, Mexico	2,500

COLD

Cold injury usually occurs either when there is a strong wind or you are wet through or both. It can occur rapidly if you are injured or immobilised at high altitude. Minor degrees are common if you expose your skin to the sun when climbing in the hills during the day, then become chilled overnight. Blood becomes diverted to the inflamed skin so further reducing your body temperature.

Symptoms and signs that your body is seriously cooling down resemble drunkenness. They also include a feeling of intense cold, uncontrollable shivering, tiredness and listlessness. When walking it takes increasing effort to keep going and to avoid stumbling. There may be slowness in responding to the comments and questions of companions, angry or confused responses, or denial that anything is amiss. Be alert for any companion who has stopped, rested or apparently fallen asleep.

Signs of *frostbite* are intense pain at the site – usually cheeks, chins, ears, nose, hands and feet, followed on the cheeks, by hard whitening of the skin. Check any area which has registered pain as soon as possible.

Frostnip which can quickly lead onto frostbite, causes numbness and whitening of the skin, most commonly on the cheeks which may pass almost unnoticed.

Prevention

Keep dry – by wearing a waterproof outer layer, which will also protect against the wind. Prevent excessive sweating on the inner layer – best done by wearing cotton or string underwear, and leaving the neck and wrists open for ventilation, unless the temperature is far below freezing.

Wear several layers of clothes, each one being comfortably larger than the one below so that there are no tight fits. In this way layers of air are trapped so increasing insulation, and any dampness from outer or inner layers tends to spread less. Cover your head with a hat or scarf, protect your hands.

Set up a 'buddy system' where each of a pair watches out for warning signs in the other.

Treatment

Treatment of hypothermia consists of *gradual but sustained rewarming without delay*. Remove your companion from the wind or wet, take off any wet clothes, give a warm sugary drink and share your body heat in a sleeping bag. Do not give alcohol. Supervise for at least twenty-four hours.

Treat *frostnip* by rewarming, e.g. with warm breath in a gloved hand, but do not rub the skin. Treat *frostbite* by protecting the affected part and by evacuation and rewarming as soon as prolonged rest and medical care are available. Give appropriate painkillers.

HEAT

Your body normally takes fourteen to twenty-one days before it becomes used to a hotter climate. During that time the sweat glands become more efficient, and water and salt regulation improves. In these first three weeks risks and discomfort are greatest, but they may occur at any stage especially in the elderly, or those who are overweight or unfit. Risks are increased during strenuous physical activity in the sun, or in a hot and humid atmosphere.

There are two forms of illness caused by heat – one common

and easily treated – *heat exhaustion*, and the other rare and much more serious – *heat stroke*.

You can largely avoid both of these by following commonsense precautions: don't 'rush the tropics', wear loose-fitting cotton clothing, and a hat in the sun. Keep up your fluid intake and add salt to your meals; avoid exercising when the climate is too hot or humid. Treat malaria and diarrhoea correctly.

HEAT EXHAUSTION

This results from heavy sweating with the loss of fluid and salt, matched by inadequate fluid and salt replacement. The symptoms include lethargy, headache, faintness, and inability to concentrate. If salt loss predominates these features are more severe and muscle cramps occur: if water loss predominates there is marked thirst. The temperature (which should be checked) remains normal, and sweating still occurs, though signs of dehydration may occur.

Treatment is to rest in a cool place and take large amounts of oral rehydration solution, fruit juices or drinks to which salt has been added (see page 51).

HEATSTROKE

This occurs when the body is no longer able to control its temperature, which starts to rise, often rapidly. It is caused by fatigue of the sweat glands or severe lack of fluid. The skin becomes hot and dry and the patient becomes confused, and may lose consciousness. Heatstroke is an emergency and the person should be undressed, placed in the shade and sprayed with water, fanned and taken to hospital. Malaria can cause or worsen this condition.

SUNBURN

On returning from an assignment overseas, friends and acquaintances may show more interest in your sun tan, or lack of it, than in what you have actually been doing. Most expatriates soon realise that the sun is largely something to be avoided, except when carefully controlled. However sunburn is still common, both on holidays, outdoor work projects, or in the case of children, forgetful or distracted parents.

Too much sun, apart from causing sunburn in the short term, also leads to an increased risk of skin cancer in the long term. You should therefore *both* avoid getting sunburnt *and* any prolonged exposure which ages and damages the skin. 'The bronzed beauty of today is the wrinkled prune of tomorrow.'

As far as holidays go, you should be able to develop a modest tan without unduly damaging your skin provided you take a few commonsense precautions.

Guidelines for skin protection

Remember that:

• The power of the sun increases rapidly the nearer you get to the equator, the higher the altitude at which you are living, and the nearer it is to the middle of the day. Most burning takes place between 10a.m. and 3p.m.

• Reflecting surfaces *greatly* increase the burning power of ultra-violet light, meaning you can still burn on a cloudy day. This applies to sand (beaches and deserts), sea and snow. Ultra-violet light strongly penetrates water meaning you are not safe swimming or snorkelling. Shirts and blouses obviously help, but may not entirely protect either.

• Expose yourself gradually – starting with fifteen to twenty minutes and increasing by a few minutes each day. If the skin starts to look red or feels sore go into the shade at once.

• Apply sun lotion every one to two hours and again after swimming or heavy exercise. If your skin is very fair start with a protection factor of 20 to 24, otherwise 15 to 18 will be sufficient. Preferably use a water-resistant brand if you intend to swim, snorkel or do water sports. Use a cream which protects against the two main forms of UV light, UVA and UVB. Uvistat and Soltan do this.

• If you frequently have to walk or work in the sun, wear a wide-brimmed hat, or use an umbrella or headscarf, keep your arms covered and apply suncream to your face and lips. These precautions will also help to protect against the long-term effects of the sun. Finally – don't forget your arm resting out of the vehicle window.

• Children on tropical beaches or swimming pools, especially if fair or freckled *need careful protection*. It is sad when a child's only memory of the holiday-of-a-lifetime is the agony of sunburn. Spend time explaining why protection is important so that you are working together on the problem.

• Babies should never be placed in direct sunlight.

• Certain parts of the body need extra protection, especially the lips, any depigmented patches or areas only rarely exposed.

• Some medicines increase the tendency of the skin to burn, especially tetracyclines and certain diuretics. So do certain cosmetics.

• *Treat* severe sunburn with calamine, rest and aspirin (those over 12) or paracetamol. Keep blistered areas clean. See a doctor if the burn is very severe, or blisters start to get infected. Avoid the sun until the skin is thoroughly healed.

SNAKES, INSECTS AND OTHER BITING CREATURES

SNAKES

Serious snake bite is rare amongst travellers. Comparatively few snakes are poisonous and more often than not only manage to inject a small amount of venom. Even if venom has been injected, serious symptoms usually take hours, not minutes, to develop. A poisonous bite will usually show two fang marks, quite separate from a row of small tooth marks, which are not dangerous (see diagram opposite).

Prevention of bites

By following a few rules snake bite can almost always be prevented. Snakes attack when provoked, virtually never attacking if you keep still. If living in areas where poisonous snakes are known to live, follow these precautions:

• When walking outside, especially in long grass or thick undergrowth, carry a stick to beat the path in front of you. Wear boots or strong shoes and trousers. At night in addition carry a torch.

• Keep the grass and other vegetation short around your house.

• Never put your hand into holes, onto or under rock ledges or any anywhere you cannot easily see if a snake is lurking.

• Avoid climbing trees or rocks covered in dense foliage.

• Take care walking under overhanging trees or bushes.

• If camping in an area where snakes are common, try to sleep on a bed or raised platform, at least one foot off the ground.

• Avoid swimming in rivers matted with vegetation, in mangroves or muddy estuaries (sea snakes).

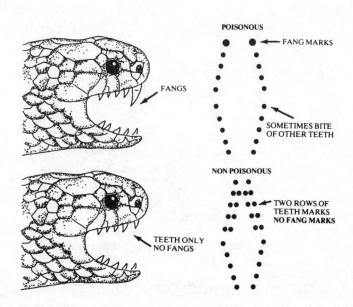

• Inside the house check dark corners before reaching into them.

• If you come across a snake stay absolutely still.

• Never handle snakes even if they appear harmless – or dead.

Symptoms of snake bite

Everyone who thinks they may have been bitten by a snake is extremely anxious, and signs of anxiety mimic the symptoms of certain forms of snake bite. Signs which suggest that venom has actually entered the body include the following: bleeding from nose, areas distant from the bite or blood-stained vomit/dark urine; swelling spreading up the limb from the bite; drooping of the eyelids; difficulty swallowing or breathing; slow, irregular pulse or falling blood pressure.

Treatment

Give maximum reassurance and keep the affected body part *as still as possible*, preferably below heart level. Any remaining

venom should be wiped off the skin. In the case of a bitten limb apply a firm, broad bandage along its entire length, splinting the limb if possible. Only if this is really impracticable should you apply a tourniquet. This must be tight and be slowly released after twenty or thirty minutes under medical supervision.

Go to the nearest health facility known to have antisnake venom, taking the dead snake if possible, but not handling it directly. The anti-venom should be given intravenously by an experienced health worker only if there are definite signs of envenoming as mentioned above. Adrenalin must be on hand in case of an allergic reaction. Pain should be treated with paracetamol, and not aspirin which may worsen any bleeding tendency.

You should avoid cutting, sucking, electric shock therapy and traditional remedies such as the 'black stone'.

LEECHES

These are common in jungle areas and monsoon forests, usually lying in wait by the path. The writer, when inexperienced, once had fifty leeches attached at one time when trekking in monsoon Nepal. Leeches are dangerous only when attached in numbers over a period of hours when they can cause marked loss of blood.

Prevent leeches from biting you by wearing stout footwear and trousers tucked in at the ankles to boots or thick socks. Apply a *DEET*-containing insecticide to your skin and soak trousers and socks in *DEET* or permethrin before going out. Salt or industrial spirit will cause a leech to detach itself in anguish but the wound bleeds and itches for some time afterwards and occasionally gets infected if the biting part of the leech remains in the skin. Avoid swimming in forest lakes or rivers where water leeches are known to occur.

VENOMOUS FISH

Some fish have poisonous spines which can detach if you brush against them (e.g. when diving in coral reefs), or tread on them (as with sting rays in shallow seas). Fragments of tentacles can become painfully embedded after brushing against poisonous jellyfish, with potentially fatal results in the case of sea wasps and box jellyfish.

Prevent these hazards by getting expert local advice when swimming, snorkelling or scuba diving in unfamiliar areas. Avoid sting rays by shuffling rather than stepping in sandy water where they are known to occur.

The *symptoms* of envenoming include sudden severe pain, swelling, and in more serious cases diarrhoea, vomiting, sweating or difficulty breathing which spells urgent transfer to hospital.

First aid treatment is important. Immerse stings from rays or other fish in water as hot as you can stand. In the case of spines and tentacles from fish and jellyfish remove these with tweezers having urgently applied vinegar or dilute acetic acid first.

Sea urchin fragments can easily become embedded in the sole of your foot in tropical seas. Smaller ones gradually absorb and disappear; others can be removed by forceps after paring down the skin, having first softened it with salicylic acid.

SCORPIONS AND SPIDERS

These usually bite only if annoyed. Avoid reaching into unlit corners, and shake any shoes before putting them on. Don't walk barefoot in the house or anywhere else if scorpions are known to be present. Check your bedding.

In scorpion-infested areas, camp sites should be checked and cleared of scorpion tunnels before pitching tents.

Most scorpion bites are very painful; only a few are dangerous: Mexican, Brazilian and north African species being the most notorious. An injection of local anaesthetic (e.g. lignocaine 2%) or a strong painkiller can be given. Children or anyone seriously affected should go to hospital.

Spiders, with a few exceptions such as the Black Widow or Redback, are rarely dangerous. Prevent and treat in the same way as for scorpions.

BEES AND WASPS

There are two potential dangers for travellers. The rare attack by swarms of bees, usually in thundery weather (run fast or dive into water). More common and easier to deal with is the single sting if you are hypersensitive to bees, wasps or hornets.

If in the past you have had a severe reaction to a sting or have developed progressively worse reactions take and keep with you at least two minijet self-injectable adrenalin kits and wear a Medic Alert Tag (arrange through your local chemist or phone 0171–833 3043).

Nettle rash, swelling of the lips or tongue, or wheezing are signs you should use adrenalin straight away. In addition take a double dose of an antihistamine (e.g. chlorpheniramine, Piriton).

FLEAS

Fleas are small jumping creatures 2–3mm long, compressed sideways. They cause itchy bites, often in children, and are found anywhere on the body but commonly around the ankles. They are usually found in association with domestic pets.

Prevent flea bites by applying flea powder regularly to dogs and other domestic mammals. Where living accommodation is infested with fleas, carry out the following: apply flea powder to all areas where fleas are found; sleep at least two feet above floor level having first checked your bedclothes, body clothes and body surface for fleas. Treat any animals: be patient – flea populations detached from their animal hosts eventually die out.

JIGGERS

These fleas are found in many parts of Africa, and parts of South America. They cause symptoms by burrowing into the toes or feet and forming pea-sized swellings which may ulcerate.

You can prevent them by wearing good shoes or boots when

walking in areas where they are known to occur. The treatment is to ask someone experienced in dealing with them to remove the jigger with a sterile needle.

LICE

Lice are crawling insects 2–3mm long found in the scalp, body hair or pubic region (crab lice).

They lay eggs and the empty eggshells known as nits are dandruff-like objects attached firmly to the hair shafts. Head lice are very common in the tropics, often affecting expatriate children.

Treat all forms of lice with Lindane 1% lotion. Rub in well, leave for four minutes, shampoo, and comb through before drying; repeat if necessary. An alternative preparation is Malathion 1% shampoo following maker's instructions.

In applying either of these preparations, avoid eyes and mucous membranes. For head lice apply only to the head, for body lice apply to all body hair except the scalp but including the beard.

Lice are *prevented* by good personal hygiene and by avoiding intimate contact with those infected – not, of course, easy to ascertain in advance!

Lice on clothing can be dealt with by washing the clothes in hot water (over 55°C) or sealing clothes in a bag for two weeks when all the lice will die out.

TICKS

If you notice a small nodule or bump on your skin not apparently there a few hours or days before, this could be a tick. They attach themselves to the body, usually after you have been walking through vegetation or been in close proximity to animals. Ticks feed on blood, gradually enlarging and eventually falling off.

They can however cause disease (tick encephalitis, tick bite fever, typhus and Lyme disease). Where they are known to occur check your skin, or that of your companion, each evening. *Remove* them by tweezers using the following technique: grasp firmly, press inwards, rock slowly from side to side, and gently detach taking care not to leave the head behind.

Prevent tick bites by using insect repellent on the skin, or soaking trousers and socks in DEET or permethrin. Tuck your trouser legs into thick socks.

MITES (causing scabies)

Mites are tiny creatures causing this common skin condition, frequently caught by expatriate children who go to a local school or by health workers and others in close contact with the local population. *Symptoms* include severe itching, especially at night. Scabies quickly spreads to other family members.

Treat it by applying Lindane lotion or cream, or Benzylbenzoate lotion overnight to cover the whole body from the neck downwards, making sure all family members who may be infected are treated at the same time. All sheets, blankets, linen and clothes with which your skin has been in contact should be washed in hot water and dried if possible in full sun. Itching may persist for up to two weeks after the scabies is cured. If it still continues treat again or see a doctor.

BED-BUGS

These usually bite at night, often leaving a scattering or a line of intensely itchy bites on exposed parts of the skin. They also hide in benches, for example at railway and bus stations, leading to a line of bites behind the knees.

Prevent them by choosing clean accommodation, applying an insect repellent at night and placing your bed in the sun during the day, dusting it first with an appropriate powder. *Treat* bites by *not scratching* them and with an antihistamine by mouth (e.g. chlorpheniramine or terfenadine, see page 206).

TUMBU FLY (mango fly, putsi fly)

If you develop the symptoms of a painful boil, especially if living in tropical Africa, or more rarely South America, make

sure there is no maggot inside it. This first betrays its identity
by two black dots near the boil's surface. The larva enters the
skin from eggs laid by tumbu flies on clothes which have been
left outside to dry.

This condition is *prevented* by hot-ironing all clothes left outside
to dry in those parts of the tropics where it is common, or
better, drying clothes inside.

It is 'cured' by placing a drop of oil on the boil overnight and
gently squeezing out the maggot. The squeamish do best to
wait in the next room.

WAYS OF SURVIVING
AN OVERSEAS ASSIGNMENT

There is supposed to be a grave in India with the following epitaph: 'Here lies the body of a person who tried to hurry the east'.

Perhaps the main secret of coping with a new country is to identify an appropriate pace to life, and then adapt your personal rhythms accordingly. This will be based on your own happy mean between the laid-back fatalism of the local population on the one hand, and the reasonable goals and expectations of your job, expedition or travel plans on the other.

Here are some suggestions:

THE CLIMATE

When first landing in a tropical airport children sometimes wonder why the pilot hasn't turned the aircraft engines off, only to discover that the blast of hot air comes from the country, not the plane. It takes two to three weeks before your body partially adapts to the new temperature, and longer if the climate is humid. Even then you are unlikely to be able to maintain the pace of life that you are used to. Allow much longer than usual for normal physical and mental activities.

When first arriving in a hot country you will obviously lose large amounts of fluid through perspiration. This means you must replace both the fluid and the salt by drinking large amounts, more often, and adding salt to your meals. A good alternative is to make up your own rehydration solution (see page 51). Although this is normally used to replace fluid lost in diarrhoea, it can be very reviving during a long, hot tropical day, especially in the absence of safe, soft drinks. You should avoid using salt tablets.

Wearing appropriate clothes can also help you to acclimatise.

They should be *loose fitting*, so allowing air to circulate; *absorbent* so allowing you to cool more easily (cotton and silk are the best materials), and *pale in colour* so they reflect rather than absorb the heat. Acclimatisation is slower in the elderly, the pregnant, the overweight or if you are very exhausted. Men acclimatise slightly quicker than women, in whom undiagnosed anaemia can slow the process further.

LANGUAGE

There is nothing so frustrating as not being able to communicate with the people whom you have left home and luxuries to live alongside. Only the lucky few can fully learn a new language on the job. If you are going on an overseas assignment of say two years or more you must ensure adequate time for language study before starting any official tasks. During this time language learning should take priority over everything else. Even after this phase is over language slots must be built into your timetable so you are able to continue studying. It is worth discussing this in detail with your sending organisation at an early stage, so that everyone has the same expectations. A Linguaphone or BBC course can help *before you go*, as can getting hold of a phrase book or user-friendly text book.

CULTURE SHOCK

Usually on first arrival you are carried along by the excitement of seeing new places, meeting new people and all the exotic sights, sounds and smells. This phase, unless illness hits early, may last from a few days to a few weeks. Except for some short-term travellers, a time of disillusionment and frustration usually sets in as cultural delights get replaced by annoyance at things not working, the food you like not being obtainable, people speaking an incomprehensible language and dirt, dust, heat and noise without end.

At this point it is easy to take a psychological dip and get irritated, depressed, lonely and homesick. However, if you learn how to cope with these phases, which will recur from time to time during your time abroad, you can eventually adapt to your host country the way it is, good and bad, and hold the positives and negatives in an integrated balance.

SOME SURVIVAL TIPS

● *Take time off/out.* Set as a priority time for personal rest and relaxation. For those living overseas this will need to be at the very minimum one day per week, one long weekend in six, four weeks per year. In refugee and civil war situations the weekend should become a week taken completely off-site.

If there is no obvious place to escape to, and nothing to do when off-duty or away from work it is even more essential early on in your assignment, to devise ways of relaxing on-site and constructing a bolt-hole. Work out a system of protecting your personal privacy.

Expats who work all week, then use Sunday for church or voluntary activities are high-risk candidates for burn-out. Even back-packers and travellers will need at least one 'domestic' day per week or the delights of the road and new travel experiences will irritate rather than stimulate.

Leisure time needs to be built into your contract and the understanding of your senior colleagues – even if it may not be understood in the local culture. It also needs to be programmed into your personal and family expectations. Mothers (and fathers) of young children are a priority sub-group!

Unless you give top attention to time out, exhaustion and burn-out will eventually occur, even though it may take time to declare itself, often after a period of unproductive guilt-driven activity.

● *Have varied social contacts.* In isolated postings it is common for everyone to work, play, relax and even pray together. Sooner or later, usually sooner, relationships, and personal contentment, begin to break down.

Cultivate friendships outside your immediate circle, with local families and acquaintances, and with expatriates who hold differing viewpoints or concerns. Try to *make it possible* to take time out from the compound, campus or immediate surroundings.

• *Discover leisure interests*. Many birdwatchers and stamp collectors have first developed their interest overseas, as have mountaineers, geologists, novelists and painters. The customs, culture and art forms of many developing countries are a rich mine of interest. Board games, reading, BBC World Service, or BBC World TV, or CNN, joining or starting a Scottish dancing club, reading the *Guardian Weekly* or the *Sunday Observer* help to keep you fresh and integrated, as does watching funny videos sent from home.

• *Take part in regular sport*. Swimming is often ideal, crocodiles and bilharzia allowing. Walking, tennis, volleyball and badminton may be possible. Some expatriates even go jogging, despite the looks of surprise from the local population. Regular physical exercise, ideally at least once or twice per week, not only helps you to keep fit, but also helps to reduce stress.

• *Become a writer*! Some people find that at times of severe frustration, difficulty or excitement, adopting the mindset of a novelist or journalist can be helpful. Half-day waits in the visa office, or close shaves at an armed roadblock or street demo become prime source material.

• *Accompanying spouses*. For partners with no specific job description, expatriate life can at times become frustrating and boring. Caring for the children and the home may in large part be carried out by others, friends and relatives are on another continent, and you may have no official job or role. Moreoever your partner may be busy and fulfilled (and therefore insensitive to your needs), or very frustrated with an assignment that is not working out (and therefore needing you on whom to offload aggro).

Apart from following the commonsense tips above, one or two other things may be helpful in this situation:

• As far as possible define, discuss through and clarify your likely role overseas before you go, with your sending agency, field leader and partner. You may be able to draw up a specific job description, task or appropriate expectation. If your role is to be left vague, or you are to 'wait and see how things develop' this should be through an informed, planned decision and not simply by default.

• Develop your own outlets away from home, cultural patterns and visas allowing. This may mean voluntary help in the local community – through a church, voluntary organisation, school or hospital. Many have discovered that their contribution in the informal sector is just as valuable as if they had gone out with a specific job description or role.

• Invite friends from home, or elective students and expatriate volunteers living nearby to stay or share meals.

• Determine to become really proficient in the local language. This is the best way of reducing social isolation.

• Learn about a new subject, either informally or by correspondence, or through the Open University (if living in the European Union).

• Learn to play a musical instrument.

• Resist the delights and dangers of too much booze, whether local or brought in from outside (see page 119).

• Be open with your partner, who will need to understand the realities of your own life, and the way you feel. Be proactive in establishing time off as a couple and as a family.

PROFESSIONAL UPDATE

For many working or serving overseas, professional opportunities can be exciting and challenging. Keep notes of interesting or significant discoveries, events, cases or ideas. Make sure you receive professional journals from home. When on home leave try to fit in some professional update, course or conference. Consider writing a paper, or travel article or book.

MEDICAL FACILITIES IN DEVELOPING COUNTRIES

These will vary greatly between one country and another, and between cities and rural areas. The best may rival our teaching hospitals, the worst be places to avoid. Although many excellent doctors and hospitals are to be found, you will probably be alarmed by the crowding, lack of hygiene and difficulty in communication. Two further hazards are the mercenary attitude of some doctors – and less-than-brilliant nursing standards. Here are some survival tips:

● Minimise the need to see doctors by being healthy, fully immunised and well prepared before leaving. While overseas set up a sensible lifestyle, try to avoid road accidents (see page 85), take antimalarials, use insect repellent and sleep under a bed net where indicated.

● On arrival (or preferably before) find out about the nearest reliable hospital, doctor or medical facility. Resident expatriates and the British Embassy or consul are good sources of advice, and your own organisation may well have details. Knowing what is available (and what is not) is essential, especially if you have young children. Many countries have western, or western-trained doctors in their academic institutions, mission hospitals or private practices.

Medical databases listing good health facilities worldwide are now in existence and your medical adviser may be able to access this.

● Take your own needle and syringe pack in case you need an injection and gently insist that this is used, unless facilities are known to be reliable. This is especially important in tropical Africa. Also take any other recommended kits such as AIDS protection kits, and a first aid pack.

● Women should be aware that doctors in any country may occasionally fail to follow considerate or ethical practices. Be prepared to say No to an examination you feel is unnecessary or inappropriate.

● For guidelines on pregnancy abroad see pages 123–38.

MEDICINES AND INJECTIONS IN DEVELOPING COUNTRIES

There is enormous variation in the availability of useful medicines. Although essential drugs may sometimes be hard to obtain, brand products are often in abundance. In most of

Asia and Latin America and in the larger cities of Africa many medicines are available without prescription from roadside pharmacies.

Before buying medicines overseas:

• Check they are made by a reputable company, preferably a multinational, and that they look genuine. Fake drugs are common especially in west Africa and south Asia.

• Check the expiry date.

• Check the generic or scientific name (usually found somewhere on the bottle or packet, though in small print) to make sure it really is the preparation you want.

• Avoid preparations which contain steroids (e.g. prednisolone) unless this is definitely what you need. Never use eyedrops with steroids unless prescribed by a doctor skilled in eye diseases.

• Avoid blood- or serum-based products, including locally-made gammaglobulin. They can spread HIV infection.

• Avoid injections, intravenous glucose and other widely used remedies *unless really indicated*. In many countries health workers, from doctors to traditional practitioners, use injections even for mild self-limiting illness. Often no treatment is needed at all, or medicines by mouth will be just as effective. If an injection is essential go to a reputable health worker, and provide your own needle and syringe, unless you know a sterile, unused syringe will be used.

• Avoid routine vitamins and tonics, unless prescribed or medically recommended.

ALCOHOL

In some countries, or particular communities, alcohol is forbidden or strongly discouraged. If this is the case it is only worth accepting a drink if this is both legal and acceptable with those amongst whom you live and work.

A greater problem is often the free availability of alcohol

including home brew – which added to tiredness, loneliness or stress can bring to light a past, or new, drinking problem.

It is worth setting yourself high standards, as prevention is far easier than cure. Consider keeping a drink diary if you find it hard to keep your drinking under control. In this you list out *when, where, how much and with whom* you drink each day of the week.

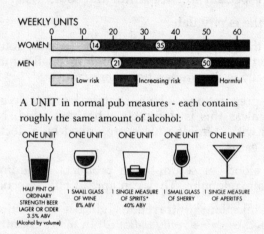

WEEKLY UNITS

	0	10	20	30	40	50	60

WOMEN (14) (35)

MEN (21) (50)

Low risk   Increasing risk   Harmful

A UNIT in normal pub measures - each contains roughly the same amount of alcohol:

ONE UNIT   ONE UNIT   ONE UNIT   ONE UNIT   ONE UNIT

HALF PINT OF ORDINARY STRENGTH BEER LAGER OR CIDER 3.5% ABV (Alcohol by volume) | 1 SMALL GLASS OF WINE 8% ABV | 1 SINGLE MEASURE OF SPIRITS* 40% ABV | 1 SMALL GLASS OF SHERRY | 1 SINGLE MEASURE OF APERITIFS

Sensible rules include: never exceeding the recommended limit (21 units per week for men, 14 units per week for women), keeping three days per week alcohol-free, practising ways of saying No, never getting drunk, drinking alone, or drinking in the morning. If this means avoiding mixing with certain people, so be it. If you ever feel the problem is getting on top of you, tell someone appropriate and ask for help before it becomes known in the community or passes beyond your control. In the UK there is a National Alcohol Help Line, also known as Drink Line, on 0345 320202.

SECURITY

Although this varies widely, security is a problem in many parts of the world, as are the dangers of robbery, rape, kidnap and getting caught up in a local disturbance.

A few commonsense rules can greatly minimise your risks:

PERSONAL POSSESSIONS

Avoid ostentatious dress and gadgetry. Travel with as little cash on you as possible. Wear a money-belt, preferably inside your clothes, or use a tubigrip to keep cash or tickets on the inner side of your leg. Watch your possessions with great care in crowds, in public transport especially night trains, and on beaches. Be on guard for pickpockets especially in well-known tourist areas. In areas where mugging is common consider keeping a small amount of local currency, dollars or pounds where you can easily hand them over.

PERSONAL SAFETY

Keep a low profile, understandably difficult for blondes in Africa or giants in East Asia. Avoid dark or lonely areas in city or country. Keep to well-worn routes. Try to travel with a local resident who knows the best routes to take and how to cope with any difficult situation. Try not to use maps in public, but study the route in advance of setting out. Avoid excessive alcohol. Don't pick up unknown travellers if driving. Stop at road blocks, and do what you are asked. Avoid arguments and political discussions. If you find yourself on the edges of a disturbance or demonstration, beat a hasty retreat. You can get detailed advice on the safety of travel in any country of the world by phoning the Foreign Office on 0171–270 4129/4179.

DOMESTIC SAFETY

Assess the likely risk of robbery, armed or otherwise, and take appropriate precautions. This may mean keeping a guard dog, building a perimeter fence, having an intercom with another nearby resident, or employing a watchman. Consider using a time switch for lights or radios, calling a loud good-bye as you leave an empty house, fitting security locks and window bars, and keeping a whistle handy. The fitting of a 'foghorn' on the roof is traditional in some African countries.

Thieving is often opportunistic meaning you should not leave things lying around your garden or an open house, and that you should secure all doors and windows with care whenever you go out or at night. Only employ domestic staff after making sure, preferably by reliable references, that the person is of good reputation.

HOTEL SAFETY

(Double) lock your room, keep valuables with you, and retain your key when leaving the building. Don't leave precious things lying around in your room. Remember that your passport may have a high value on the black market.

SPECIAL GROUPS

PREGNANCY

Parents-to-be often wonder if it is safe to travel or live in a developing country when pregnant. Before deciding on this you will need to understand the level of risks for different places at different times during pregnancy. You can be helped in this by discussion with your doctor or obstetrician, and also through the guidelines which many sending agencies and companies will have available.

It is helpful to consider pregnancy overseas under three separate though related headings:

- Safety of travel during pregnancy;
- Safety of living in a developing country when pregnant;
- Safety of having a delivery overseas.

SAFETY OF TRAVEL DURING PREGNANCY

The act of travel during pregnancy carries some additional risks, owing to the greater likelihood of fever, dehydration, accidents and distance from good health care, when away from home.

If you do have to travel in the first three months, try to arrange at least one antenatal appointment before going abroad, at which time you can discuss any concerns you have with your doctor. You may just be able to fit in your first scan.

The middle three months (mid-trimester) are generally the best time to undertake a journey. In this way you can complete basic antenatal investigations including blood tests and scan before you leave, and be in place for any problems which may arise towards the end of the pregnancy.

You should think carefully about travel if any of the following apply to you. They would not necessarily stop you but you should discuss them with your doctor:

(a) You have had a *medical condition* adding to the risk of pregnancy. These would include heart disease, diabetes, significant anaemia, asthma or chronic lung disease, previous deep venous thrombosis or pelvic infection. It might also include any other serious or long-term illness, especially if you are taking medication for it.

(b) You have had a *problem in a previous pregnancy*. These would include a previous actual or threatened miscarriage, ectopic pregnancy, known complication of childbirth, Rhesus incompatibility or raised blood pressure. Include any other condition which caused you to have extra appointments or treatment in your last pregnancy.

(c) You have *problems in your present pregnancy*. These would include any vaginal bleeding, marked abdominal pain, raised blood pressure, presence of twins or a known low placenta.

SAFETY OF LIVING IN A DEVELOPING COUNTRY WHEN PREGNANT

This will vary greatly depending on the country and your exact location.

Although most overseas pregnancies will pass without difficulty, if problems do arise or a tragedy does occur you will want the reassurance that you took an informed choice based on the knowledge of possible risks. It is therefore worth considering what the commonest risks are:

Miscarriage. There is an increased risk of this in the tropics because of fever, especially malaria, and severe dehydration.

If you do have a miscarriage, especially after twelve weeks, medical facilities such as those for Dilatation and Curettage (D and C) may be less reliable – and less hygienic. Safe blood may be harder to get in the rare event of needing a transfusion.

Malaria, especially malignant malaria which is common in sub-Saharan Africa and south-east Asia, increases your risk of anaemia, premature labour, miscarriage and stillbirth. The baby may be born with malaria. You can reduce the danger by taking strict precautions, but some risks both for mother and baby still remain.

You should avoid travelling in western Cambodia and the Thai border areas with Myanmar and Cambodia when pregnant as the only effective treatment is not safe in pregnancy. You should think carefully before living in any country where there is a high risk of chloroquine-resistant malaria.

Medicines Many medicines, including most treatments for diarrhoea, bowel infections and worms, are best avoided in pregnancy, meaning you may need to delay treatment until the baby is born. A bewildering number of drugs is available in many developing countries, either by prescription or over the counter. You should only take medicine both if it is essential, and you have checked it is harmless to the baby.

Premature labour. Although in the absence of malaria this is little more likely in Honduras than in Hampshire, access to adequate treatment, such as safe blood for the mother and extra support for a premature baby, is greatly reduced.

You can minimise health risks during pregnancy by trying to set up an ordered lifestyle, taking regular exercise, and allowing more time than usual for rest, relaxation and routine tasks. Avoid high-altitude trekking, scuba diving, horse-riding and skiing.

SAFETY OF HAVING A DELIVERY OVERSEAS

There is potentially a greater danger from complications at the time of delivery in a developing country, unless you are within access of a known centre of excellence. Generally facilities both for routine and for emergency care are less reliable. You will need to make an informed choice, not through a romantic haze of optimism, but based on a cool look at what would happen in the worst scenario.

The following are suggested *minimum* requirements for an overseas delivery:

• A maternity unit, easily accessible at all times of the day or night and at all seasons, with twenty-four-hour cover from an experienced doctor able to carry out forceps and vacuum deliveries and Caesarian sections.

- High standards of hygiene, fully trained midwives and the guaranteed use of sterile instruments.

- The ready availability of safe blood from a trusted donor with the same or compatible blood group.

- Resuscitation facilities for the newborn.

- The absence of any serious pregnancy-related problems in this or previous pregnancies, including Rhesus incompatibility.

- A personality which can cope with the added risks and anxieties of having a delivery away from your home country, with its high-tech back-up and family support.

- A partner or family member who can give practical support at the time of delivery including overseeing travel arrangements.

In coming to your decision you should visit the maternity unit, meet the doctor and midwife likely to carry out the delivery, and thoroughly check out the facilities. Make sure the doctor(s) is not away for long periods of time (or is a golf fanatic), or is not about to go on home leave. Talk with other expatriates who have had local deliveries, and with the medical officer of your organisation.

Even if the minimum requirements are in place, the balance may still be tilted in favour of you coming home if:

Either this is your first delivery;

Or you are working in a country where HIV disease is common;

Or there is political instability.

If you decide against going home you may opt to move nearer the capital or large city two weeks or more before the delivery date. Alternatively you might decide to move to a nearby country with better health facilities.

If you do not feel comfortable about having a pregnancy overseas you should make sure you discuss this with your sending agency or medical adviser. Equally if you are very keen to start a family make your wishes clear.

After the birth of the baby make every effort to breastfeed, not bottle feed, but don't allow yourself to be guilt-ridden if this really isn't possible.

AIR FLIGHTS AND PREGNANCY

Most international flights will be unwilling to carry a passenger known to be thirty-five weeks pregnant or beyond, but many domestic flights make a cut-off point at thirty-six weeks. Check the exact regulations with the airline concerned and leave a margin of two weeks in case of last-minute changes of plan or cancellations.

Air travel is generally safe in pregnancy. Make sure you keep your fluid intake up, and avoid alcohol. Your feet may swell more than normal. In order to prevent clots in the legs walk around at least once every hour and avoid sitting in a cramped-up position. Eat a fibre-rich diet throughout pregnancy and especially at the time of air travel. Travel sickness may affect you more than usual. Avomine is effective and safe.

Check the details of your travel insurance as most policies will not cover delivery or complications of pregnancy.

IMMUNISATIONS AND ANTIMALARIALS IN PREGNANCY

Although the risk of foetal damage from any vaccine given in pregnancy is extremely rare, like all medical decisions risks and benefits have to be matched up.

Plan your immunisations plenty of time ahead so that you can still have essential vaccines before you become pregnant. Tetanus, and gammaglobulin for hepatitis A are safe, other vaccines are best postponed. Immunisations are safe when breastfeeding.

Make sure you have had measles and rubella immunisations; if in doubt, a blood test can tell if you have protection.

If you are going to a malarious area you must take antimalarials as well as strict precautions to avoid bites (see also pages 58–80).

RHESUS INCOMPATIBILITY

There is a risk that Rhesus negative mothers who carry Rhesus positive children can have their own blood sensitised by their baby. The mother then develops Rhesus antibodies which can adversely affect future babies.

The use of Anti D immunoglobulin helps to prevent Rhesus illness in the newborn and is recommended for Rhesus negative mothers in the following situations:

• For use within seventy-two hours of birth. If facilities abroad allow the blood group of the newborn baby to be tested and the baby's blood group is confirmed Rhesus negative, an injection of Anti D immunoglobulin is not necessary. If the blood group is positive, or testing is not possible, Anti D immunoglobulin should be given to the mother, whether or not any Anti D was given during pregnancy.

• For use within seventy-two hours of a miscarriage, or threatened miscarriage including vaginal bleeding.

• For use within seventy-two hours of external version, antepartum bleeding, trauma to the abdomen, amniocentesis or chorionic villus sampling.

• In some countries guidelines recommend that Rhesus negative mothers should receive Anti D immunoglobulin at twenty-eight and thirty-four weeks of each pregnancy. This is not currently recommended by British experts.

The vaccine should be kept between 2° and 8°C but can be taken in hand luggage during a flight provided it is refrigerated on arrival. It should not be frozen. Rhesus negative women who may have further pregnancies overseas should consider taking Anti D globulin with them.

CHILDREN

Most children enjoy living overseas, and many find returning home to the UK after several years in a tropical country harder than going out in the first place. Where problems do arise overseas they are usually caused by illness, times of separation, or parents so involved in projects and programmes that their children do not get the quality time which they need. This can of course happen just as easily in the UK.

BEFORE LEAVING HOME

Give kids the vision! Enable older children to share 'ownership' of what you as a family will be doing. Involve them in your arrangements, excite them by what you will be involved with. In doing this be careful not to raise false expectations or expect them to share the burden of making important decisions.

You can prepare very young children by selectively reading aloud about the country you are going to, showing them photographs, slides, films or videos. Older children can be encouraged to do a project on the country, ideally at school. If the class teacher is involved and makes this a class project it can help to maintain links between children and their classmates over the coming months.

If you can meet up with a family who has recently been to the place you are going to, so much the better, especially if they have children.

Usually it is worth keeping plans to go abroad under wraps until they are reasonably firm. Continue normal school and family routines for as long as possible.

Children of all ages will need continuity with home throughout their time overseas. Encourage them to keep up friendships and write regular letters. Favourite toys, cuddlies and books can make all the difference to the happiness of children during their first weeks overseas. Make sure there's space for toys, books and that favourite teddy. Keep a back-up trunk of other favourites not taken overseas for opening at home when you come back on leave.

When overseas try to arrange visits from friends, relatives and grandparents. These, if appropriately timed and not too long, can be enriching times and give a valuable sense of continuity to children.

If your assignment is remote and long-term take extra sets of baby clothes of progressively larger sizes, and take with you appropriate birthday and Christmas presents for at least a year ahead.

Some children worry about whether they will like the food overseas. Reassure them and take care that meals and meal-times are enjoyable, and that you don't introduce too many new tastes and smells all at once. There is some value in alternating European-style and local-style meals.

EDUCATION OVERSEAS

Before confirming an overseas assignment do careful research into school options, and assess how suitable they will be for the likely duration of your time overseas. You will need to talk to other families who have had recent experience of the area you are going to.

A local school has many advantages for younger children as it helps them to feel part of the scene. These good points may be overshadowed by variable quality of teaching and a sense of cultural isolation unless children are accepted as ordinary members of the class. Home schooling is an option which suits some families well, but not others. Check it out carefully, looking at different systems, preferably one compatible with British educational requirements.

Children of secondary school age may do better at international schools, even if this means boarding. Boarding is hugely popular with some children, loathed by a few, and agreeable to most. If children do board, visit as often as possible, and be sensitive for any stress or unhappiness which may arise from bullying, loneliness, overstrict teachers or rare cases of abuse. Most international schools offer a first-class education.

If children board in the UK make sure they have guardians which both they as well as you approve of and like. During holidays be especially careful to make them feel wanted and affirmed. This will mean pre-planning so that one or both parents have time free. Children who go to boarding school may subconsciously equate this with rejection, meaning that holidays or special visits are of great importance. Decisions by longer-serving expatriate families regarding when to come home are quite critical and need to be thought about in advance on the basis of well-researched data.

HEALTH CARE BEFORE LEAVING

Children will need appropriate immunisations, including BCG, and some courses started in the UK may need to be completed overseas. DPT, polio, and measles, are likely to be available, others may need to be taken. Discuss this with your travel health adviser.

Remember to start antimalarials one week before leaving. Make sure you know your children's blood groups. Arrange medical, dental and eye checks on older children or if your sending agency or company requests these.

ON THE PLANE

Many children will feel sick going to the airport, so give your preferred antisickness pill (see page 27) at the correct time before leaving. Planes are exciting to start with, but especially for younger children can become frustrating after a time. Make sure you tell the airline that you have children so they can book a suitable seat, and accommodate or provide a cot. Take with you a supply of small, appropriate toys, books, puzzles and treats which can be produced at magic intervals to treat, bribe, or prevent boredom.

Children get very thirsty on planes – make sure they get plenty to drink as unrecognised thirst can make them bad-tempered. You can be sensitive to the needs of others on the plane without hedging your own children in with too many prohibitions.

LIVING OVERSEAS

Allow plenty of time at the beginning so you can get to know and understand your new environment together. Encourage your children to make friends with local children and families but at their speed, not yours. Some children will react to the new situation by withdrawal and shyness. Give them space to develop relationships in the way and at the speed with which they feel comfortable.

If more serious withdrawal occurs give additional home support and less contact with unfamiliar or frightening aspects of the culture around them. They may in addition be missing friends at home but may not always mention this.

After a period of withdrawal gently encourage new friendships with other children and introduce them to enjoyable aspects of life in your new location to encourage them.

If there are local customs which frighten young children – cheek-pinching in south Asia is a common example – explain that this is the normal way of greeting children and is not an act of hostility.

Monitor your children's experience of the schools they go to, making sure they are not getting academically behind compared to their contemporaries at home, and also that no unusual customs or patterns of discipline are causing unspoken anxiety.

You can help family bonding by making sure that each member of the family is familiar with what the other members do and the places where they work and study. In many cases children will take an active and informed interest in the work you are involved with if you share it with them and give them a sense of ownership and involvement. If you travel out from home-base as part of your work, try to take the children with you from time to time.

Make plenty of time for family activities. Many children brought up overseas retain lifelong memories of family picnics, visits to safari parks, tropical beaches and mountains, or just simple family days together. Holidays can take on new dimensions overseas, so never jettison them in favour of worthy schemes and work schedules. Workaholics often come into their own when abroad – to everybody's disadvantage, especially their children's.

Finally: when travelling with small children take special care they don't get lost while they (or you) wander off to investigate the latest sight or sound.

FEEDING CHILDREN OVERSEAS

It is worth breastfeeding for one or even two years. Apart from all the other benefits it makes diarrhoea less likely.

Try to prepare feeds yourself for the baby using carefully washed utensils, rather than leaving it to the cook, houseboy or ayah, unless you have carefully trained them. It is better not to feed any reheated food to very young children (see pages 35–8).

Give children and especially babies *boiled* water. Make sure there is a cool supply at all times so that children when arriving home thirsty, don't have to make secret visits to the tap or well.

Because of the heat, children may have less appetite than in the UK. This means a balanced diet is especially important. Include a good source of protein, either eggs, meat, fish or lentils, as well as regular fresh fruit and vegetables. Keep a growth chart for children under 5 to monitor weight gain. These are usually available from the local clinic or health centre – it does not matter too much if they are not in English. Take seriously any unexplained fall in weight or flattening of the curve.

ILLNESSES ABROAD

By leaving Basildon or Basingstoke you do not necessarily leave behind sore throats, earaches, snuffles and coughs. As a parent you may worry that ordinary symptoms are caused by extraordinary illnesses. Usually, with the exception of malaria, they are not.

However you should take special note of the following:

● *Fever*. This may be caused by malaria (see below), or by any common childhood illness. High fever should be treated by undressing (under a mosquito net), tepid sponging, and paracetamol. High fever or any fever which persists for more than eight hours, especially in a malarious area, means you should see a doctor. If this is not possible treat for malaria as any delay can be dangerous. You must then seek advice if symptoms are not definitely improved within twenty-four hours. Avoid aspirin in those under 12 years old (see also pages 175–7).

● *Headache* if accompanied by vomiting or stiff neck. With or without a rash this spells immediate referral to a doctor: it may be meningitis (see page 185).

● *Cough or breathing difficulty.* Beware of pneumonia which you should suspect if the respiration rate reaches fifty or more per minute or if there is indrawing of the ribs or flaring of the nostrils on breathing. See a doctor if possible and start antibiotics, such as cotrimoxazole (Septrin, Bactrim) or amoxycillin at the correct dose for age. Asthma is common in children and may start for the first time when you are overseas. Any severe attack of wheezing needs skilled treatment quickly.

● *Abdominal symptoms.* Only the luckiest child (or adult) will escape diarrhoea. Start ORS at once (see pages 50–1); breastfed babies should continue to take breast milk. Giardia is common in children and persistent diarrhoea or flatulence in any member of the family may be caused by this. Threadworms causing itchy bottoms are common and all family members over the age of 1 should be treated with mebendazole (one, twice daily for three days) if any family member has symptoms. Abdominal pain, especially if it persists, is accompanied by fever and settles into the right lower abdomen, could be appendicitis. See a doctor.

● *Infected cuts and grazes.* In hot, and especially in humid climates, minor injuries easily get infected. Clean all breaks in the skin with care, use antiseptic cream and keep covered with a light non-adherent dressing, frequently changed until the skin is healed over (see page 194). Boils are common.

● *Scorpion and snake bites.* Scorpions like dark places. Teach your children to check their slippers and shoes before putting them on, to take care when putting their hands into boxes or into any dark place. If snakes are common set up a family drill on how to avoid them and deal with them (see page 104).

● *Dogs and animals.* A family pet is often a vital member of the overseas family. Make sure that the dog's rabies injections are always up-to-date (see page 47). Actively discourage your child from ever approaching, touching or stroking an unfamiliar dog, or any other unknown animal.

● *Sunburn.* The combination of sun, light or absent clothing, excited children, and distracted parents spells danger. Allow your children's skin to acclimatise gradually, starting with fifteen minutes' exposure only, using high-factor sun lotion. When swimming or on seaside holidays take along an old shirt with long sleeves and stay in the shade during the middle of the day. If sunburn does occur, blame yourself and not your child, apply calamine and watch out for any infection (see page 102).

• *Accidents.* These are amongst the greatest hazards overseas. A few days after arrival make a tour of the house and its environs and assess it creatively for any obvious or potential risks, never forgetting the family medicine shelf, probably groaning under a heavier weight than back home. Check the cooking area carefully, making sure that hot handles cannot be easily reached and pulled off the stove. Crossing roads in a developing country is a skill which children should only acquire at the side of an adult, especially if driving is on the right, you live in a city, or are visiting one from up-country.

• *Sleep problems.* Children, like adults, may suffer from disturbed sleep when going to a new environment, especially if it is hot, or there are unfamiliar smells and noises. Heat, the whining of mosquitoes or prickly heat may add to the problems. In addition it is easy for children to be stimulated, or alarmed by new and bewildering experiences. Often the best remedy is to allow the child to talk and play even if it is beyond normal bedtime. Extra contact with parents may be all that is needed. If this and other remedies fail, or if you yourself are desperate for sleep, then promethazine (Phenergan) or trimeprazine (Vallergan) for a few nights at the recommended dose for age can help to break the cycle. Occasionally this stimulates rather than sedates. If you have children 3 or under, give a trial run in the UK, then take a small supply with you.

• *Medicines.* For all but the shortest trips it is worth taking one or more courses of antibiotics, an antihistamine, sickness pills etc (see Appendix A). Make sure you avoid medicines that are unsafe in children and use the correct dose for age. In a malarious area never run out of prophylactics and keep a standby with you for treatment (see page 74).

RETURNING HOME

Periods of leave at home need to be so arranged that children do not feel squeezed out or of secondary importance. Make sure they see the people *they* want to, and do at least some of the things they want to do. Help them to understand the way their own country ticks so that when they finally come home they are not strangers in their own land. In the case of an extended leave one or two terms at school can be very beneficial.

If your children have had more than one or two years abroad it is not advisable to bring them straight back into the first GCSE or A-level year without a prior year to get adjusted. Teenagers usually find re-adaptation to their home country difficult and will need the most favoured opportunities possible for re-entry. Schools in the UK will need to have explained to them in detail the background, both academic and cultural, from which your children have come, otherwise they may be seriously misunderstood. Church youth groups and Sunday schools as well as the wider family, including grandparents, can be very helpful in giving children added security.

Returning home for good can be bewildering for the whole family, not least for children. Peer pressure in schools, especially during teenage years, is strong, and wearing current styles of footwear and knowing the right fashions, pop songs and slang can greatly reduce isolation and embarrassment. The more you have encouraged children to remain bicultural overseas the easier will be their eventual reintegration.

HEALTH ON RETURN

Along with other family members children should have a medical examination if they have lived in a developing country for longer than a year. This should include a stool test. It is sensible for all family members over the age of 1 to take a course of worm medicine – mebendazole, one, twice daily for three days. If children have swum in areas where bilharzia is known to occur they should have a blood test (or urine/stool test). Malaria commonly occurs weeks or even months after coming home. Untreated malaria in children is *dangerous*. If you have been in a malarious area do report any unexplained fever at once and ask for a blood smear.

SUMMARY

Children usually thrive overseas. They will usually adapt without too much difficulty to the sights, sounds, and even the dangers of a new country. Parents can help this process by being relaxed, flexible, friendly and sensitive. Involve your children, seeing them as key members, not only of the family but of the programme you are involved with. If you find this difficult it may mean you are too busy, need more holidays or more frequent home leaves.

DISABILITY

Provided you choose your destination and means of transport with care, physical handicap does not disqualify you from serious travel. Inhabitants and hosts in many countries are often very helpful. An 80-year-old relative of the writer recently made a three-week journey to a remote part of western China three months after a severe stroke had left him completely paralysed down one side, and without speech for two weeks. His secret? – determination, a sensitive travelling companion and careful preplanning with airlines and accommodation.

A wheelchair should be robust, lightweight, as narrow as is comfortable, and able to be folded up. It should be well tested before the journey, and accompanied by a few simple repair tools. Battery-driven chairs are probably best avoided. A strong and considerate travelling companion for all but the hardiest is essential.

By prior arrangement with the airline assistance can be provided at all stages of the journey, a suitable seat procured in the plane near the disabled toilet, and the wheelchair accommodated on deck. For many airlines provision tends to be all or nothing. This means if you say you are disabled you will probably be supplied with full assistance at each stage of the journey. However, check out with care any special claims made by airlines or hotels.

During the flight it is important to exercise or massage the legs to prevent clot formation. Those on regular diuretic pills should continue to take these. All medication should be kept in your hand luggage to avoid anxiety and in case of delays.

Travellers with severe hearing disability will need a companion who can pass on advice and information, and interpret needs to hosts overseas.

Information about wheelchairs can be obtained from Wards Mobility Services on 01892 750686 and on any aspect of travel for the disabled from The Disabled Living Foundation, 0171–289 6111 and RADAR, 0171–637 5400. Consider reading the book *Nothing Ventured*, a collection of travel vignettes by disabled globetrotters. See 'Further Reading', page 228.

DIABETES

Many diabetics manage to travel with little danger, provided they are well controlled, well advised and well supplied. However you should discuss any trip outside Europe, or any overseas assignment, with your GP or specialist. If you use insulin you would need to be in reach of good medical facilities, preferably in the company of an informed companion. Have a doctor's letter with you giving details of the insulin dosage, and wear a Medic Alert bracelet.

Before *flying* inform the airline at least seventy-two hours ahead that you are a diabetic and ask them to serve you appropriate meals. If you are crossing time zones you should discuss a detailed action plan with your diabetic adviser. Normally you would be advised to stay on home time until you arrive at your destination, then gradually alter your injection times by two or three hours at a time. Test your urine or blood frequently both while travelling and for some days after arriving, altering your insulin dose accordingly. Running 'a bit high' is unlikely to cause any harm for two or three days.

In cases of *illness, fever or diarrhoea* you will probably need more insulin and should test your urine, or blood, at least four times daily. See a doctor *early* if you become less well or vomiting persists. As a diabetic you should take extra care to avoid preventable illnesses, in particular malaria and diarrhoea. Take special care of your feet, treating any fungal or other infections immediately.

Take all necessary *supplies* with you until you have personally checked out their availability where you are going. This includes insulin, needles, syringes and testing equipment. Divide your supplies between two cases and remember to keep all insulin in your hand luggage as the hold will freeze. While overseas keep your insulin in the non-freezing part of the fridge, or in as cool a place as possible, out of direct sunlight. Insulin that has been above 25°C for longer than a month may lose its effectiveness.

Always carry a form of *sugar* with you in case of hypo attacks. If going to a remote area or prone to attacks also take glucagon. Make sure your travelling companion knows how to recognise hypo attacks, and what to do about them. They may come on very rapidly while travelling though they are uncommon during actual air travel.

If you are a *non-insulin-dependent diabetic* continue testing as you would at home, remembering there may be slight changes owing to differences in food and climate. It is important to keep near your target weight and to be regular with any tablets you are taking.

Further details can be obtained from the British Diabetic Association, 10 Queen Anne Street, London WIM OBD (0171–323 1531). They publish details of insurance schemes, advice for tourists and availability of health care and supplies in over seventy countries.

SECTION 3

WHEN YOU RETURN

ILLNESS ON RETURN HOME

On getting back home you may continue to have medical symptoms or concerns about your health. This is more likely if you have been living in a remote or humid location, and if you have been in close contact with the local people. Countries in sub-Saharan Africa, south and south-east Asia are perhaps the most likely to leave you with a legacy of fevers, diarrhoea, weight loss or other symptoms.

Those who have been on shorter, hurried trips abroad, especially if working for hard-pressed aid agencies, not infrequently arrive home exhausted or unwell.

ILLNESSES WHICH SHOW THEMSELVES ON RETURN

Some illnesses may show themselves for the first time after you get home, while others may have started abroad but become worse or more obvious when back in this country. Important illnesses to be on the look-out for include the following:

Fever/malaria. A sensible rule is to assume that after returning home from a malarious area any fever is malaria until proved otherwise. This is especially important in the first four weeks when malignant malaria commonly occurs, but benign forms may recur for months, occasionally years after returning from the tropics. Sometimes malaria can occur for the *first* time after returning home.

If you develop a fever or symptoms which you think could be malaria, follow the advice given on page 75. Although fever may have a variety of causes *it is dangerous to ignore symptoms of fever after returning from a malarious area*. Sometimes a mild virus, or even a cold may trigger malaria, and symptoms are often atypical without the classical phases of shivering or sweating. Dengue fever, usually caught in south Asia or Central America, can mimic malaria; so can typhoid.

Diarrhoea. Attacks of diarrhoea which started overseas may continue in the UK. Symptoms occasionally occur for the first time. There are many causes including dysenteries (bacterial and amoebic), Salmonella, Campylobacter and Giardia. The last often causes persistent diarrhoea with flatulence. Diarrhoea usually disappears without treatment but you should see a doctor and take a fresh stool specimen if *either* it persists for longer than ten days after returning home, *or* if there is any blood or mucus in the stool. Continue to report symptoms until either your stomach has returned to its normal pre-travel state, or you feel suitably reassured.

If certain organisms such as Salmonella, Shigella or Cryptosporidium show up on your stool test, you may be asked to have three clear tests before being allowed back into full social circulation. This especially applies to schoolchildren, but practices vary from one part of the country to another.

Persistent diarrhoea, especially after returning from south Asia, may be a sign of malabsorption, in which case there is usually weight loss and frothy, floating stools. It is often associated with milk intolerance. This is easily treated but you must report your symptoms to a doctor, preferably one with tropical experience.

Sometimes repeated bowel problems abroad can trigger an irritable bowel syndrome (IBS) – a common and benign condition with irregular motions and abdominal pain. Again this should be diagnosed by a doctor rather than by yourself.

Remember that diarrhoea or bowel symptoms after you get home may have nothing to do with your travels – see a doctor if abnormal symptoms persist.

Worms of various sorts may first come to light on return home (see pages 182–4).

Cough or chest symptoms. Chest infections often hit expatriates during or just after their return home. If this is the case you should see a doctor, who will probably give you antibiotics. Make sure also that you report any cough that persists for more than a month (see pages 166–7).

Skin problems. Report any unusual skin symptoms. Groin

itch, athlete's foot and other fungus infections are common. Persistent rashes, sores, ulcers or suspicious moles must be checked, as should any roughened skin patches in long-term tropical residents (see page 197).

Bilharzia. If you have had any contact with fresh water in areas where this is known to occur you may later develop symptoms. Katayama fever (acute schistosomiasis) causes fever and usually wheezy cough, itching and diarrhoea. It needs treating without delay. Bilharzia can also produce blood in the urine or stool – or not give any symptoms at all (see page 162). Tests may only become positive three months (or longer) after you get infected.

Persisting ill health, weight loss, or unusual symptoms. If in doubt check it out. Ill health of any sort starting during an overseas trip or persisting after return should always be investigated.

AIDS and HIV infection. If you have been involved in health care, or had any other risk factor for HIV you may want an HIV test on return. Very few employing organisations insist on this at the present time and the choice is yours.

Many people worry about jeopardising future insurance cover. Having an HIV test is extremely unlikely to affect your premium provided you are able to write down your reason for having it as a non-recurrent occupational health risk whilst overseas. If however your lifestyle puts you at risk you should discuss this further with your medical adviser.

An HIV check can be included as part of your tropical check-up either by your GP or in a tropical diseases centre. Alternatively it can be carried out at an STD (sexually transmitted diseases) clinic, probably the best place if you are worried that you may have picked up another form of STD in addition. Before having an HIV test carried out you will be given appropriate counselling and have the right to full confidentiality.

Psychological problems. Coming home can often be a time of stress, especially after a long or difficult assignment. A tropical check if the doctor has time can be a good opportunity to talk about any bad experiences. Certain events overseas are known to make adjustment more difficult or to increase the risk of flashbacks or other unpleasant symptoms. For this reason we would recommend an opportunity for psychological debriefing (see page 148).

Career blank. It is very common after taking a year out or after exciting or significant experiences abroad to feel really confused about what you should do next. In this case it is worth arranging a career interview either with your local careers' service or privately (see page 212).

HAVING A TROPICAL CHECK-UP

WHO CARRIES THEM OUT?

If you are unwell or have symptoms you should be carefully checked, preferably by someone with experience of tropical illnesses. This could either be with your GP, university health centre, NHS tropical diseases unit, or other centre specialising in travel medicine (see Appendix D). For any NHS referral you would normally need a letter from your GP.

WHO SHOULD HAVE ONE?

If you are well with no symptoms, opinions vary as to whether a medical is necessary. Many people are worried that they may have some hidden illness which will declare itself with mortal results, months or years later. Although this is rarely the case there are certain groups of people who benefit from a medical when they return from overseas:

• Anyone with persisting symptoms.

• Anyone residing in a developing country for more than six months who has not had regular access to good health care including a reliable laboratory.

• Anyone whose style of travel has placed them at special risk. This includes those on remote locations, overlanders, some overseas volunteers backpacking during their holidays, or those working in famine, refugee or civil war conditions.

• Anyone with a risk of contracting serious local diseases such as bilharzia, river blindness or Chagas' disease.

- Anyone suffering from stress or depression or who feels they would benefit from counselling.

- Anyone whose employing organisation recommends a medical.

WHAT DOES IT CONSIST OF?

A tropical check-up usually takes this form: detailed questioning about any illnesses experienced, areas visited or points of concern. An examination which includes listening to the chest, checking for any enlargement of spleen, liver or lymph glands, feeling the abdomen, a careful check of the skin, and examination of the ears, eyes and mouth.

At some centres (including InterHealth) there is also a chance to talk through any difficult overseas experiences.

Investigations usually include a stool and urine test, and where appropriate a haemoglobin and full blood count (including percentage of eosinophils – a useful marker of parasitic infections). Tests can also be arranged on the liver and for bilharzia, filaria, Chagas' disease (parts of South America only), HIV or any other condition which you or your doctor are concerned about. Chest X-rays and ECGs are only rarely necessary. The most useful 'tropical tests' are stool examinations and eosinophil counts.

If you are returning overseas you can also have your hepatitis A antibodies checked unless you have had hepatitis A vaccine. If these are positive you have immunity and will not need immunisation with hepatitis A vaccine or gammaglobulin. If you are a health worker or have previously had a course of hepatitis B immunisations you can have your blood titres measured to see whether you need a booster.

It is worth remembering that a single negative stool test does not mean your gut is necessarily free of parasites. If symptoms continue you should have at least three stool tests, preferably fresh, taken to the lab. within one hour of production. Many doctors in addition recommend that all those returning from an assignment in developing countries, either permanently or for prolonged leave, should take a course of mebendazole for worms (one, twice a day for three days). In addition those coming from areas notorious for amoeba or Giardia, e.g. south Asia, Sudan and Mexico, sometimes take a course of tinidazole or metronidazole, followed by diloxanide to eradicate amoebic cysts (see pages 52–3).

PERSONAL DEBRIEFING

Any difficult, dangerous or frightening experience overseas, either short-term or long-term, may have various effects which you may only feel after returning home. They may make adjustment more difficult, lead you to feel anxious or depressed, or cause gloomy thoughts or disturbing dreams which don't seem to go away. Occasionally they can lead on to a more serious condition known as Post-traumatic Stress Disorder (PTSD) or bring to light underlying tension or conflict which may have been present before you went overseas. Many of these problems can be greatly lessened by a chance to talk about any bad experience in a free-ranging debriefing interview on return home. If you have been on an assignment your sending organisation will normally arrange an operational debrief (make sure you have one).

In addition however it is helpful to have a 'psychological or personal debrief' when you can talk about your feelings, fears and experiences.

The best time to do this is within one or two weeks of returning home. These debriefs usually consist of a one to two hour unthreatening interview with a trained counsellor, when you can talk freely about any aspect of your overseas experience. They are strictly confidential and are distinct from counselling, though at the end of the session you may mutually agree that a series of counselling sessions might be helpful.

If you have been with a group of people who have all suffered a similar traumatic experience a group debriefing for two to three hours can be very helpful. Ideally this should take place as soon as possible after the incident.

Debriefing is best thought of as a chance to talk about 'normal reactions to abnormal situations'. We suggest you consider arranging one of these if you come into one of the categories below:

• You have been working in a situation of famine, war, conflict or danger.

• You have experienced actual or threatened kidnap, rape, assault, armed robbery or other frightening experiences.

• You have had any serious or long-standing personality conflicts with colleagues.

• You have had an assignment which has been cut short, has been especially difficult, or has not worked out at all as expected.

Finally it is worth mentioning that some people find their religious faith challenged or threatened by experiences overseas, especially those which have involved seeing severe or mass suffering. In this case it is really worthwhile seeing a spiritual counsellor, chaplain, pastor or minister for prayer and discussion. Many people find that once they develop a well thought through 'theology of suffering' their faith can grow rather than falter (see Appendix D).

GPs, DENTISTS AND OPTICIANS

REGISTERING WITH A DOCTOR

If you handed in your medical card on going overseas you should now reregister with a GP. If you are not sure how long you will be staying at your address you can register as a temporary resident for up to three months, during which time you enjoy full NHS access. When registering permanently, your doctor or the practice nurse will want to see you for a brief medical, but this does not take the place of a tropical check-up. If you have previously been registered with either the same practice or a different one it may take at least six weeks for your old notes to be retrieved. As a temporary resident your previous notes would not normally be sent for.

NHS ELIGIBILITY

On return to the UK you will be entitled to NHS treatment if:

Either:

You have lived in the UK for ten or more continuous years in the past and, since living overseas, have either visited the UK at least every two years *or* been entitled under your contract to have done so, *or* have a contractual right for your fare to the UK to be paid by your employer at the end of your contract.

You are a visitor to the UK who has been 'ordinarily resident' in the UK for six months or more.

Or:

You are a visitor to the UK and there are reciprocal health arrangements in the UK for citizens of your country (e.g. members of the EU).

You are a visitor and your illness has only developed since your arrival in this country. In this case you will be eligible for free treatment with a GP, hospital outpatient or accident and emergency department, but any inpatient treatment you would probably need to pay for.

In some of these instances you may need to stand on your rights. For further details see: *NHS Treatment of Overseas Visitors*, Department of Health 1988. This is due for revision in 1995.

SEEING A DENTIST

At the time of writing an increasing number of UK dentists are no longer taking on new NHS patients. For this reason it will often be worth seeing a dentist known to you from before or who is known to any relatives with whom you are staying. In addition a list is available from InterHealth of UK dentists with a particular sympathy for those serving abroad.

SEEING AN OPTICIAN

As a general rule it is worth having an eye check at least every five years and more often if you wear glasses or have any personal or family history of eye disease including glaucoma.

Eye checks are no longer generally free nor is a green form necessary from your doctor. If there is a history of glaucoma in your immediate family you are entitled to have your intra-ocular pressures measured free. You should have this done every five years over the age of 40 in any case. Let the optician know if you have been taking chloroquine regularly for more than six years.

BEING REFERRED TO A SPECIALIST

Those coming home on short leave are having increasing difficulty getting specialist referrals within the National Health Service, largely because of the new-style market orientated NHS.

If you need a specialist referral follow this procedure:

See your GP as soon as possible after getting home, or if you know your GP, write from overseas; explain the problem and your limited timescale, being sure to mention if you are serving with a charitable organisation. If there is likely to be a delay write a courteous note to the consultant to whom you have been referred, marked for personal attention; ask the medical adviser of your sending agency or company to write a supporting letter to either your GP, the consultant or both. If an appointment still cannot be arranged, consider seeing the consultant privately.

REVERSE CULTURE SHOCK

We shall not cease from exploration
And the end of all our exploring
Will be to arrive where we started
And know the place for the first time.
T. S. Eliot

Even if you are one of the lucky ones who can quickly adapt from one culture to another and feel as comfortable after ten days back in Taunton as during your ten years in Timbuktu it may still be worth reading this.

THE PROBLEM

A surprising number of people do get thrown by the effects of re-entry, especially after any long, difficult, inconclusive, or intensely meaningful experience abroad. It may seem even more of an issue than the culture shock you experienced, or didn't experience when you first went abroad. You may have assumed that the comforts of home, indulgence in your favourite luxuries, and friends eager to hear of exploits in remote corners of planet earth are bound to make you feel good.

And when you first arrive home, are met at the airport, and start to recount exciting experiences as the hero, or tramp returning home, you probably *will* feel pretty good. But after a while this gradually seems to change. For no apparent reason you may start feeling listless, anxious or depressed; you don't want to get up in the morning; you start losing your enthusiasm, even your self-confidence; you feel angry at the materialism, decadence and pettiness of people's lives; you feel confused about yourself and about your future. Perhaps for the first time in your life you find yourself crying in your room – or snapping in public. What can possibly be the matter?

Probably nothing. You have the normal condition of reverse culture shock. You have left a country and its people whom you have come to love and appreciate. You have left a job or travel experience which despite its frustrations was often fulfilling – and sometimes exciting. You have lost a role, and a clear place in the scheme of things. Now you are mourning the loss of all this, you are missing acutely the good friends, favourite places and significant experiences. 'Last week at this time I was . . . now I am looking out of a rainy bedroom window in Birmingham.' If you have ever lost a close friend or relative you may recognise the similarity of some of your feelings now.

Apart from sadness at what you have left behind, you may be shocked by what you find at home. As an outsider coming in to land, and then acting as a detached observer, you can see the way the country really is, the aloofness of the British, the stifling materialism, and the apparent indifference of the people around you to the real issues of the world. You may feel like a messenger from outer space with insights and understanding which no one will listen to. If you are a Christian you may start to identify with the way Jesus may have felt when he swapped his residence in heaven for a home on earth.

Further, you find yourself in a dilemma. On the one hand you realise a need to reintegrate into the society you've returned to, and on the other you do not want to compromise your enriching experiences and sense of enlightenment by becoming like the people whom you feel you have moved beyond. Staying an outsider may be painful but you wonder whether it isn't better than taking on the colours of the people around you and thereby compromising the value of your overseas experience. It seems as though you have moved on in your personal development whereas your friends seem either to have stayed the same or moved in another direction.

As if this isn't enough it seems that even your friends have changed. To start with, they all seem so busy. They no longer seem to talk about important things (did they ever?). Even those who should know better ask banal questions about why you are not more suntanned. They quite forget which country you have been living in and for reasons of ignorance or embarrassment ask hardly any questions about the real things you have been doing, or too many about certain things you would like to forget. They seem more interested in the latest fashions in trainers than in the concerns of the poor. And when you do find someone genuinely interested you are so relieved that you go on talking for too long.

Life too is very bewildering. Take shopping for a start. Why are there so many things on the shelves? Is it morally justified for supermarkets to sell forty-seven different types of breakfast cereal? And how come the prices have gone up so much? Before leaving for overseas you felt at home in the streets, now you no longer do so. Even going to the post office requires undue concentration to avoid saying something silly or coming away with the wrong denomination of stamps.

You may become annoyed or intimidated by friends, family and acquaintances continually asking what you are going to do next, or enquiring when you are going to settle down – as though your overseas experience was some blip which nice Brits don't go on talking about.

Perhaps you first went abroad because one chapter in life was drawing to a natural close, or because you felt a strong urge – or call – to do so. Now you are home, this chapter has closed, but the pages in the rest of the book seem blank. Careers? New jobs? You are hardly able to cope with yourself – how can you possibly cope with making decisions, writing a CV, being interviewed, starting a new course or job, earning a living?

SOME POSSIBLE SOLUTIONS

If you can identify with some or all of these feelings, relax – you're normal. If you can't, don't worry either. Those with certain personality types can cope with change much more easily than others. Of course you may feel it later.

Here are some suggestions which may help:

Recognise – and don't deny – the feelings you have. Writing them down may help. Choose good friends with whom you can share your feelings; rather than being shocked they may be relieved you are human. Make the most of the debrief with your organisation, getting anything off your chest that you need to. If you have been in a tough location or had a difficult experience, seriously consider having a personal debrief shortly after coming home (see page 148). Equally, if your relationship with a partner or spouse seems to have taken a nose-dive (common overseas and on re-entry) try to arrange some joint counselling. Try not to leave any unfinished agenda with your sending agency or company. Ask for a further session if you need it. If money is an issue or you sense that you were let down or sent out with the wrong expectations, talk about it.

Keep in touch with overseas friends and projects. There are useful things you can probably do for some time to come and this will give continuity, purpose and a knowledge you are still usefully involved. Join any group where others who have returned meet to discuss, pray, or raise support for people and projects you are familiar with. Go to any reunions, reorientation weekends or get-togethers. Keep up with friends now in the UK you have known overseas. You, and others, will benefit from setting up a bridge from your past life to your new one.

Be patient. Let the process of integration take its own, appointed time. Before you feel part of things again, it may be days, weeks, months or even years depending on your personality, how long and how deeply you were involved overseas, and how often you have been home. Gradually you will be able to adapt to the UK without feeling your overseas experiences have to be wasted or jettisoned. This will happen as you come to see people as individuals, not stereotypes, situations as dynamic and not static, and one day's challenges at a time as all you are asked to cope with. You will learn the knack of accepting the good, avoiding the bad, and recognising what you can usefully do to help bring change within the limits of your gifts and energies.

Dare to admit your ignorance about many of the things you used to know about but no longer do – how things are done, work patterns, the latest fashions, celebrities, TV programmes and political issues. You are unfamiliar with some of the customs and culture of the country you now find yourself in, so admit it, put on your social anthropology or detective hat, and find out about the strange inhabitants of your home country just like you did for the locals when you first went abroad. Wander in the shops, familiarising yourself with prices, brand names, and what is available. Make the *Radio Times* your study project. Take note of what people are wearing, what the new banknotes look like and the value of unfamiliar coins. Find a good and long-suffering friend and question him or her about things you want to find out about, especially unfamiliar words you keep hearing and that people expect you to know. Your knowledge about all matters materially trivial but socially important will grow and so will your confidence.

Join a social group where you will feel comfortable and where you have a shared interest. It may be a church, an evening class, a club or a parent-teacher association. As you become used to one group, so other situations will become less daunting.

Get some careers advice if you are unsure about your future. Your local careers service can supply you free and relevant information about courses and jobs. They can explain about retraining schemes, eligibility for further education grants and accreditation of prior learning. You are entitled to use their library, and usually their computerised list of courses throughout the UK.

Although it may help your peace of mind to know when your next job or course is going to start – and when the cheques will start coming in – don't necessarily be in too much of a hurry. Do this at your pace rather than that of well-meaning friends eager to know what you are going to do next. Get to know yourself and what you really want to do now that you are home. Your interests, outlook and viewpoint may start to change over the first few weeks – or months – you are back in the UK, especially if you have been abroad for some time. Don't necessarily take the first job that comes your way simply out of desperation. It may be better to wait until something more appropriate becomes available. In the meantime get someone to help you prepare an elegant CV which maximises the value of experiences you have had. Don't be intimidated by a period of unemployment, but do show you have used the time constructively. As an unemployed person you are in the company of many others including top executives.

Take a holiday and do the things you've been looking forward to doing. After a tough overseas assignment one month is an absolute minimum; six to eight weeks is more realistic if the assignment has been hard or prolonged. You may have been caught up in the 'Protestant Work Ethic' – enjoy the Protestant Leisure Ethic and 'the God who gives us all things to enjoy richly'. Don't take on too many assignments and speaking engagements until you have had a proper break, your slides have been developed and your family's needs have been put first. This may mean some preplanning with your organisation

before coming home, and should be based on what you know you can comfortably cope with rather than what you feel you ought to be doing. You may feel the need to have a time of personal reflection, or if a parent, time as a family – or just as a couple.

Know when to shout. If your feelings of doom and gloom persist unduly, or are very severe and if your appetite and sleep pattern become markedly disturbed, don't hesitate to see someone who can help. Some sympathetic counselling along with temporary antidepressants or sleeping tablets will normally hasten a cure. If your assignment has been especially difficult, or you have had to come home early, these feelings are more likely to affect you. It is *not* a disgrace to be 'honourably wounded' in overseas service (see page 231).

Downhill from now on or slipway to a richer life? With time and practice it is possible to build on your overseas experience whether it has lasted twelve months or twelve years. Your time abroad, whether rich and hard to leave behind, or bleak and hard to understand, will always be potentially enriching provided you integrate the experience into your personality. Who knows? – it may be the gateway for a longer or more productive time abroad in the future, the means of helping you to understand and reach those of different cultures within this country, or of making you a more complete and sympathetic person. It may even help you to introduce your family and friends to the joy of overseas travel – or service.

SECTION 4

NOTES ON IMPORTANT CONDITIONS

BACKACHE AND SCIATICA

Backache and sciatica can cause much concern to travellers. The effect of lifting heavy luggage, sleeping in unfamiliar beds, needing to restrain or carry young children, and being tense and hurried all put the back at greater risk. This can be compounded by springless buses, rickshaws striking potholes or years bumping across bad roads in vehicles with decaying seats or groaning suspension.

If you have ever had a severe back problem, slipped a disc or had persistent sciatica *you should discuss this with your doctor before leaving,* or when next back home. If necessary ask to see a specialist or osteopath. If your bouts of backache are unpredictable, severe, or slow to return to normal, give careful thought to where, and how you should travel.

Preventing backache is much easier than treating it. Follow *with extra care* the techniques you know to be important for your own back. The cardinal rules include: standing and sitting up straight, keeping your back straight when lifting, putting a small cushion to the small of your back when sitting, and doing any regular exercises you have proved to be beneficial.

One of the most important ways of both preventing and treating a bad back is to have a satisfactory bed with a firm, but not over-firm mattress. If you wake in the morning with your back worse than when you went to bed it is likely your bed is contributing to the problem. It is fine to use a soft mattress a few inches thick, provided it is on top of a completely firm unsagging wooden base. The floor is a good alternative. Treat with suspicion any spring mattress unless new.

Treating a bad back is the same in the tropics as anywhere else, though there is often little medical backup if your back finally 'goes'. Bed rest is often the only treatment available to you though a friendly physiotherapist has come to the rescue of more than one stranded volunteer. A severely slipped disc is a regular cause for repatriation.

There are certain *warning signs* which you should report at once. These include backache associated with difficulty passing urine, weakness in the feet or legs, sciatica and numbness down one leg which worsens despite treatment, and pain or numbness down both legs at the same time. Any of these symptoms may indicate that pressure, usually from a slipped disc, is building up on the spinal cord and that urgent surgery may be needed to prevent permanent damage. These severer symptoms are however rare and 'back awareness', coupled with common sense, will enable most of us to survive.

BILHARZIA (Schistosomiasis)

WHAT IS IT?

Bilharzia is a parasitic infection caused by worm-like creatures known as blood flukes or schistosomes. They live in the walls of either the human intestine or bladder, where they produce a large number of eggs. On being released, these eggs produce symptoms, before being finally excreted in the urine or stool.

Infection occurs if you swim in fresh water where snails are present. These snails discharge larvae into the water which penetrate human skin, eventually finding their way to the intestine or bladder. It takes four to six weeks or longer before any symptoms occur, apart from mild swimmer's itch (at the time of swimming).

WHERE IS IT FOUND?

Main risk areas for travellers are sub-Saharan Africa, the Nile Valley and parts of Brazil and the Far East. Lakes Victoria, Malawi, Kariba and Volta are known trouble spots, but any fresh water including lakes, rivers, ponds and irrigation canals may be affected. Slow-flowing or stagnant water, especially if snails are present, is the most likely to cause trouble. Sea water is safe, as is any water either chlorinated or stored in a snail-free environment (e.g. a swimming pool) for forty-eight hours.

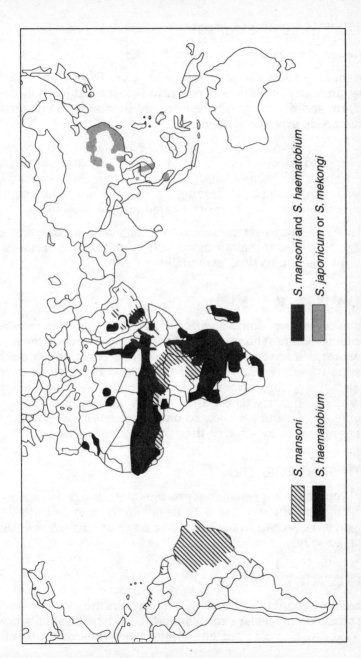

Worldwide distribution of bilharzia (Schistosomiasis) from *International Travel Health Guide*, S. D. Rose, 1994.

S. mansoni

S. haematobium

S. mansoni and S. haematobium

S. japonicum or S. mekongi

WHAT ARE THE SYMPTOMS?

The disease can take one of two courses:

(a) *Acute schistosomiasis or Katayama fever*. Symptoms which may mimic typhoid or malaria, include fever, itching, wheezy cough, and diarrhoea. The spleen and liver may be enlarged. This needs urgent treatment.

(b) *Chronic infection*. Worms live on, especially if you become re-exposed to infection. They can cause blood in the urine or semen (S. haematobium) or the intestine (S. mansoni, japonicum), sometimes leading to anaemia, and after many years to bladder cancer if not treated (S. haematobium only).

Many cases however cause no symptoms and are discovered by tests carried out at a tropical check-up. Some, but not all, symptomless infections eventually self-cure.

HOW IS IT PREVENTED?

By avoiding any contact with infected water in areas where bilharzia occurs. This means you should avoid: swimming and washing in infected water; pushing vehicles or wading through rivers; water sports in affected areas, and drinking infected water. If exposure cannot be avoided (wear waterproof boots), dry the skin immediately after getting wet, cross up-stream from villages, and get checked out (see below). The shores of lakes are far more affected than open water farther out.

HOW IS IT TREATED?

By your doctor prescribing praziquantel tablets (40mg/kg), which bring about a cure with usually only mild side-effects. If you have been at risk ask for a test on your return home (see also page 147).

TESTS FOR BILHARZIA

The most accurate test is to look for ova in the urine or stool but they are not always easily found. On a blood test bilharzia is one cause of a raised eosinophil count (one of the white blood cells). Probably the most useful test is an ELISA blood test which indicates present (or past) infection but which may take at least three months or occasionally up to six months to become positive.

BRUCELLOSIS

Brucellosis is mainly a disease of cattle, goats and sheep, and humans usually catch it through infected milk, cheese or butter. It is common in south-west Asia, and scattered cases are also found around the Mediterranean and in much of Africa. Agriculturalists, development workers and adventure travellers are at greatest risk.

Symptoms are variable and often vague, usually starting at least one month after exposure. At first there may be fever, general weakness and pain in muscles, back and joints, sometimes lasting a few weeks. Many cases then get better on their own but some continue with intermittent (or 'relapsing') fever leading to profound tiredness, further muscle and joint pain and depression. In this form it can mimic chronic fatigue syndrome, or a depressive illness.

It is *prevented* by making sure all milk (and milk products) are either politely refused or only drunk if pasteurised or boiled for ten minutes.

It is *diagnosed* by tests on blood serum and *treated* under medical supervision with doxycycline and either rifampicin or streptomycin.

CHAGAS' DISEASE
(South American trypanosomiasis)

This is a serious disease found in Central and South America, particularly Brazil, where it is spread by infected 'assassin' or 'kissing bugs' (see diagram), creatures that live in mud walls and bite at night, commonly on the face. It is a risk for aid workers, adventure travellers and volunteers who sleep in mud or adobe huts off the beaten track, especially where

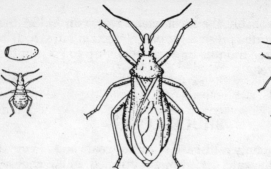

The Cone-Nose bug, also know as the Assassin or Kissing bug,
responsible for spreading Chagas' disease. (1–4cm long)

chickens are common. Chagas' disease can also be spread
through blood transfusions.

The bite is usually obvious, and the first *symptom* is a reddish
nodule at the site of the bite, often with swelling of an eyelid.
Fever commonly develops and lymph nodes become swollen.
Symptoms may however be slight or non-existent, but serious
disease, especially heart failure and swelling of the colon or
oesophagus may occur years later.

Prevention involves sleeping away from the hut or if this is
not possible in the middle of the hut away from the walls. A
mosquito net if thoroughly tucked in gives protection. Local
blankets and rugs should not be used. Search your bed for
hidden insects and apply insect repellent to your face.

Treatment under medical supervision needs to be started as
early as possible. This means that anyone who may have been
exposed or has had an unscreened blood transfusion in South
America should request an ELISA blood test at the time of their
tropical check-up.

COUGHS AND COLDS

Some people are surprised when told they can still catch a cold
when living in a tropical climate. As in the UK the majority of
colds get better on their own, but those working long hours
or following hectic international schedules frequently develop

chest infections especially at the end of an assignment or on returning to the UK.

If a cold fails to clear up after a few days and if in addition you are run down or have a tendency to *bronchitis* or *sinusitis* see a doctor and start on antibiotics such as amoxycillin 500mg three times a day for seven days or cotrimoxazole twice a day for seven days.

Pneumonia, especially in children, may develop fast, especially after a cold or when very tired. You will usually feel ill, be coughing and have pain in your chest on breathing. A respiratory rate of over fifty breaths per minute in a child is strongly suggestive of pneumonia. Call a doctor if you can and otherwise start on the antibiotics mentioned above at the correct dose for age.

Any cough that persists longer than a month should prompt you to have a medical check, as very occasionally it may be caused by *tuberculosis* (see page 202). Anyone who has had frequent or persistent coughs while working in a developing country, especially with unexplained loss of weight, should be thoroughly checked on return to the UK and should have a sputum test, tuberculin test and chest X-ray. This especially applies to health workers.

Asthma occasionally starts for the first time when overseas, especially in any children who have a family tendency for eczema, asthma or hay fever. If someone in the family develops severe or persistent wheezing consult a doctor. Any episodes in a child should be discussed on your next UK medical to make sure you are recognising and treating it in the best way. Wheezing is occasionally caused by tropical parasites.

Croup can also hit for the first time when overseas. If a child develops difficulty on breathing in, remain calm, hold your child confidently and reassuringly in an upright position, remove any pets and try to steam up the room, for example by boiling a kettle or saucepan using an umbrella or sheet as a canopy. Most attacks will gradually subside. If symptoms continue to worsen and you have a good local health facility seek medical help as soon as possible. Discuss any attack of croup on your next leave medical.

DENGUE FEVER

Dengue (pronounced *deng-ee*) is a viral infection spread by the Aedes mosquito. It is found almost throughout the tropics, especially in the Pacific Islands, SE Asia and Central America. It affects an increasing number of travellers and expatriates. Dengue tends to occur in local epidemics, often in urban areas, therefore alerting you to a probable cause for any unusual symptoms you may have.

Symptoms start with sudden fever, headache, pain on moving the eyes, and vomiting. There is frequently severe joint, muscle and back pain ('breakbone fever'). A rash often develops between the third and fifth days, usually starting on the trunk and spreading to the face and limbs. Recovery follows but a second bout of illness with further pain and fever often develops ('saddleback fever'). You may feel tired and weak for a surprisingly long time.

Dengue is *prevented* by reducing contact with mosquitoes as described under malaria. However Aedes often bite during the day so you should use insect repellents if in known risk areas. As yet there is no vaccine.

Dengue is *treated* by rest, patience and sympathy. However because it can mimic malaria it is sensible first to treat with antimalarials owing to the danger of a mistaken diagnosis. Dengue not uncommonly affects international travellers in the first week after their return from an at-risk area.

Very occasionally, and usually in SE Asia, travellers develop the more serious haemorrhagic form of the disease with bleeding into the gums and bruising of the skin, which needs urgent medical attention.

EYE PROBLEMS

Eyes are at greater risk in hot climates especially if the air is dry and dusty, or if you wear contact lenses. You can prevent most eye infections by regularly washing your face with soap and water.

Conjunctivitis is the commonest problem. The eye becomes

red, feels gritty and is sticky or stuck down on wakening. The treatment is antibiotic eye drops, e.g. chloramphenicol applied every two hours until symptoms clear.

Styes are not uncommon, especially when tired or run down. They are caused by organisms which cause boils in other parts of the body. Warm compresses can help the pain, antibiotic eye drops, or antibiotics by mouth sometimes speed up the natural healing. Styes should not be squeezed.

Contact lens wearers should discuss their trip with their contact lens practitioner, and take sufficient solution with them, using only sterilised water as additives. At the first sign of any pain or irritation the lens should be taken out for at least *twenty-four hours*. Any persistent or severe discomfort needs medical advice. Take extra contacts with you, plus ordinary glasses, plus sunglasses, which can protect against sun, dust and wind.

Glasses. Take at least one spare pair, and make a note of the prescription in case of loss. Glasses are often stolen.

Eyes and *chloroquine*. It is rare for any permanent changes to occur until a cumulative total of 100gm of chloroquine has been taken – equivalent to a prophylactic weekly dose for about six years. Experts increasingly believe that no harm will occur if chloroquine is *only* taken for prophylaxis – harmful amounts only building up if courses are in addition taken for treatment.

Early signs of reversible damage are blurring of the vision and haloes around lights. More permanent changes affect the retina leading to deteriorating vision. It is worth having regular eye checks, including examination with a slit lamp (from a medical eye centre or ophthalmologist) if you have been taking long-term chloroquine for both prophylaxis and treatment, or if you have suspicious symptoms.

Very high altitude, or polar conditions, may lead to snow blindness; prevent this by wearing goggles. Wear sunglasses for protection in very bright light.

Eye check before you leave the UK. It is worth having this done before any long-term assignment (and during regular leave).

If you are over 40 or there is glaucoma in the family have your eye (intra-ocular) pressure checked as well. You will need to ask your optician to include this.

Report any symptoms which do not clear quickly. Eyes, especially if infected, can deteriorate rapidly in a tropical climate. See a doctor, preferably an eye specialist, if in doubt.

FATIGUE AND CHRONIC FATIGUE SYNDROME (ME)

WHY AM I SO TIRED?

Feeling tired is extremely common in those living overseas (and at home). Overwork, worry, and failing to take regular time off are probably the commonest causes. You may have trouble getting on with a colleague, have frustration at work and too much, or too little, to do. You may be bored or homesick, losing sleep, or beginning to suffer from stress without realising it. If the reason is not obvious to you, ask your friends, who may have better insight than you do.

A number of physical conditions can also make you tired. Anaemia is a common one, often caused by heavy periods, not eating enough iron-rich food, having frequent attacks of malaria, or suffering from untreated hookworm or other bowel conditions.

Bilharzia (see page 162) can make you feel tired, as can brucellosis (see page 165), Lyme disease and sleeping sickness, though these are rare. Occasionally more serious, non-tropical diseases can start with tiredness, such as diabetes, and thyroid problems; so can a depressive illness.

Viruses are also a frequent cause. Two common ones are hepatitis before, during, after, and months after the illness, and glandular fever and related viruses, common in travellers and often very persistent.

If you feel abnormally tired, or it seems a long time since you had your normal amount of energy, take the trouble of having an unhurried talk and examination from a doctor who understands your culture. Various blood tests can be arranged which usually exclude serious, or treatable causes, and glandular fever is usually shown up. However many viruses are not revealed by normal blood tests.

You should not diagnose chronic fatigue syndrome in yourself, but leave this to a sympathetic doctor who has made sure there are not other, commoner causes for the way you are feeling.

WHAT IS CFS?

CFS is a puzzling and frequent illness which has become well known over the past decade. It is known by a variety of names, including myalgic encephalo-myelitis (ME), yuppie disease and the post-viral syndrome. Quite apart from its debilitating symptoms those who have it often face further problems with doctors, friends and colleagues who may be ignorant or unsympathetic. CFS patients therefore often have to run their own 'public relations bureau'. This can be especially difficult amongst expatriates where the disease appears to be common.

THE SYMPTOMS OF CFS

The chief symptom is profound tiredness and a sense of weakness or aching in the muscles, especially of the arms and legs. It has been described as 'flu minus the fever, which doesn't go away'. These features usually date from a specific time, most often from a virus infection or flu-like illness, whose symptoms persisted.

Mental exhaustion, poor concentration, memory loss and changes in sleep pattern are also common features. Vigorous or unaccustomed physical or mental exercise causes a relapse of symptoms. Because recovery is slow and cannot be hurried those with CFS often develop symptoms of despondency or less commonly an actual depressive illness.

Normally CFS is only diagnosed in those with typical symptoms which have persisted for at least six months. It is different from a simple state of chronic tiredness or exhaustion (Tired all the Time or TATT syndrome).

THE CAUSE OF CFS

CFS is commonly thought to be caused by a virus. The Epstein-Barr virus responsible for glandular fever is probably only one of several viruses which are normally rapidly fought off by the body's immune system, but which on occasions can persist, leading to CFS.

Recent research has shown that patients with typical symptoms of CFS often have a reduced number of special blood cells known as CD8 suppressor cells, thus giving scientific support to the fact that CFS is a distinct and valid physical illness (*Lancet* 21st September 1991, pp 707–11), a fact only too obvious to those suffering from it. Further research describes a biochemical way of differentiating CFS from primary depression. This gives medical evidence that CFS is distinct from depression even though the symptoms of CFS may on occasions lead on to it.

Many CFS patients are however found to have been living a stressful lifestyle at the time their illness started. Often this is through the outward circumstances of a difficult assignment, or because past problems are reactivated by the stresses of a tough overseas placement. Experience suggests that the presence of stress reduces the body's ability to fight off infection. For this reason some but not all CFS sufferers find that a course of counselling hastens their recovery.

THE DURATION OF CFS

Full recovery from CFS usually takes place but may take many months, occasionally several years.

THE TREATMENT OF CFS

See a doctor

Identify and then regularly consult a sympathetic doctor. If you think your symptoms fit into this category you should see a medic who has time, experience and sympathy with the condition, and access to laboratory tests. A hurried consultation with an uninformed and unsympathetic doctor should be avoided! This may mean waiting till your return to the UK and even then doctors will need to be chosen with care.

Some other illnesses, including some tropical diseases, can mimic CFS and it is important both medically and for your peace of mind that these are discussed and excluded, if necessary by further tests or a specialist referral.

A regular review and discussion of how you feel can be very helpful as two heads may be better than one in both planning an appropriate lifestyle and assessing progress.

Accept your diagnosis

Once CFS has been confirmed as your diagnosis accept this without guilt or shame. Recent research has confirmed the existence and 'respectability' of CFS.

You will however need to get used to explaining your illness and symptoms to others, and the use of a simple handout, or article can be helpful. The term CFS or post-viral syndrome is preferable to ME which may cause subconscious confusion with multiple sclerosis (MS), a totally different and far more serious condition.

Set up an appropriate lifestyle

Balance: The key to recovery is learning to balance input (rest, encouragement, support) with output (physical and mental exercise and other activity). This in turn depends on learning to identify and carry out the maximum activity which does not worsen your symptoms over the following days. The amount of activity takes careful working out and to start with may be surprisingly little. It will also vary from day to day.

Your output will need to include the core priorities of life plus any other activities which you are able to add in without causing excessive tiredness or delaying your progress. Overactivity, often brought on by frustration, false guilt, an obligation carelessly agreed to, or the expectations of others, can set you back days. Equally, underactivity can lead to further weakening and atrophy of the muscles.

Sleep: In the early days of CFS many feel a need or even a hunger for sleep. At this stage extra sleep or rest is an essential part of treatment. It can include a long lie-in, an afternoon nap or early night. If night-time sleep is a problem it is worth first reducing the amount of daytime sleep you take and/or gently increasing your amount of daily exercise. If that fails, consider short-term medication to help you sleep at night. As recovery starts it may be necessary to start rationing the amount of sleep you have, particularly during the day, or at least combining it with a gradually increasing exercise programme.

Work: Work and responsibility need to be removed or reduced to a level at which gradual recovery is possible. This means that reduced hours, or time away from work, is usually necessary to begin with. You will also need to avoid situations where you need to preplan activities or make diary entries which may be hard to cancel. It is hard to predict how you will feel, one day, week or month later and it is helpful not to take on irrevocable commitments. As recovery takes place you can practise a lifestyle into which a gradual return to work can be slotted. Initially this should be for a few hours, once or twice a week, with a gradual increase as energy levels allow. *Do not rush this stage*. You will need your doctor's advice and if necessary explanation to help your employer understand your needs and provide flexibility in your working arrangements.

Exercise: It is important even from the earliest days to take some exercise so as to keep your muscles in trim. Walking is obviously sensible, to which swimming and a gentle exposure to a favourite sport can be added. Absorption in a sedentary hobby, reading or studying will provide useful mental exercise.

Medication

Sometimes the symptoms of CFS and the change from a normally active lifestyle can cause clinical depression in which case antidepressants can hasten recovery. Equally, short-term, mild sleeping pills may help to break any serious sleep disturbance.

Solidarity with other CFS patients

Find others with CFS with whom you can share experiences and receive mutual support. Some but not all find the ME Association is helpful. Avoid allowing solidarity to develop into an obsessional interest in your condition. Don't allow CFS to take over your life, your conversation or to dictate your friendships. Avoid the common tendency of slipping into a negative way of thinking.

Counselling/prayer

As already mentioned this can sometimes hasten recovery, especially if you are aware of unresolved tensions. It is usually better to start counselling only when your energy levels have begun to recover. A counsellor needs to be chosen with care and should be someone who understands CFS and who is in full sympathy with any religious outlook you may have. Many have found various forms of prayer ministry helpful.

Avoid too high expectation from 'magic remedies'

Some individuals claim special diets or other inputs will help to bring recovery. Try these extras if you wish, but do not be disappointed if they are not as successful as you would hope. An increasing number of CFS sufferers claim a daily cold bath improves their energy levels.

An unexpected bonus

Many have found that being forcibly set aside with CFS has deepened their spiritual life or helped them to gain other valuable insights. Many active people need red traffic lights. A well-known autobiographical account of CFS is known as *A Year Lost – and Found*. It may however only be after your recovery that you begin to see the benefits of your illness.

FEVER

Fever in the tropics, unless mild or quickly self-limiting should be taken seriously. If living in or coming from a malarious area consider fever to be malaria, until proved otherwise.

COMMON AND IMPORTANT CAUSES OF FEVER

In practice, many fevers in developing countries, as in the UK, are caused by viruses: they usually cause short, sharp rises in temperature and rarely last more than three days.

Other familiar diseases may also start with fever including pneumonia, upper respiratory infections including tonsillitis, middle ear infection and sinusitis; tooth abscess, boils and cellulitis, appendicitis, pelvic infection and urinary infection. Blood poisoning may cause a high, swinging fever and a rare cancer called lymphoma occasionally causes recurrent fevers.

Certain *serious tropical diseases* can cause fever, and sometimes there will be few other symptoms, especially to start with.

● *Malaria* is probably the commonest (see pages 58–80) followed by

● *Typhoid* and related fevers (see page 57).

● *Hepatitis* may start with fever (see pages 179–82), as may

● *Glandular fever*, common in younger travellers and volunteers, and often accompanied by marked tiredness.

Other illnesses with fever include:

● *Schistosomiasis* (bilharzia) – common in sub-Saharan Africa (see pages 162–5.

● *Tick bite fever* – especially southern and eastern Africa (see pages 198–9).

● *Dengue fever*, usually of 'saddleback' type (see page 168).

● *Typhus* – trekkers in south-east Asia, rash present.

● *Sleeping sickness* – visitors to game parks, agricultural workers in E and W Africa (see pages 197–8).

● *Meningitis* – usually accompanied by severe headache, stiff neck, no time to lose (see pages 185–6).

● *Dysentery*, with bloody diarrhoea (see pages 48–55).

● *Amoebic liver abscess* – severe pain in the liver (see pages 52–3).

● *Tuberculosis* – recurrent evening or night fever, usually with cough (see page 202).

● *Lassa fever* – severely ill, usually with ulcerated sore throat and muscle pains, rural areas of west Africa, get home fast.

● *Heatstroke* (see pages 101–2).

DEALING WITH FEVER

It is important to find the cause for *any* very high fever or one which persists or recurs, remembering that children often spike high fevers with simple viral infections. If possible you should consult a doctor, and meanwhile cool the patient by undressing and giving cool fluids and paracetamol. This is especially important in children, despite the subconscious urge of many to cover with blankets.

If you are in a malarious area (or have recently come from one) see a doctor or health worker within eight hours and get a blood smear. If this is not possible self-treat for malaria (see page 71).

If there is no rapid improvement, then typhoid becomes more likely and you should treat for this, ideally by using ciprofloxacin 250mg (two, twice daily for seven to fourteen days), or cotrimoxazole (two, twice daily for seven to fourteen days) as these will deal with many other common causes of fever as well, including some pneumonias, urinary infections, and bacillary dysentery.

Suspected liver abscess can be treated by a full course of metronidazole or tinidazole (see pages 52–3).

If you or your children are not quickly responding to treatment see a doctor. If you have had severe or recurrent fevers abroad, especially if these have been undiagnosed, it is important to have a tropical check-up as soon as possible on your return.

GYNAECOLOGICAL PROBLEMS

These can be a particular worry overseas because of the reluctance to accept medical advice from unknown doctors. Before leaving for any long overseas trip all women between 25 and 65 should have a cervical smear (pap smear), except possibly those who have never had a sexual partner. It is worth checking on your smear result by phone. Smears should be repeated every three years if normal and according to your doctor's advice if not fully normal.

PERIOD PROBLEMS

When travelling or going to live in a strange place periods may get lighter, or stop altogether, sometimes for months. This is very common and no action needs to be taken, unless pregnancy is a possibility, or if you or your friends notice that you have lost a lot of weight.

Periods may also become irregular, abnormal or prolonged. If such problems persist you should see a doctor. If this is not possible, and you are definitely not pregnant, it is possible to take the combined oral contraceptive pill (for example Eugynon 30, Norinyl 1 or their equivalents) at a dose of four tablets a day for seven days. The period should stop during treatment and come again within the week after finishing the seven-day course. You should only do this if you have recently had a clean bill of health and can see a doctor if abnormal bleeding is not cured by this treatment.

To delay a period take the combined oral contraceptive without pill-free gaps, but you should only do this for two or three cycles.

It is worth reporting any prolonged, heavy bleeding as soon as possible whenever it occurs not least because of the increased risk of needing a blood transfusion.

Also check any persistent changes from your normal cycle when you next come home.

Finally: it is better not to be menstruating during wildlife safaris, or while swimming where sharks may be lurking.

VAGINAL DISCHARGE

This is often commoner in the tropics especially in hot and humid conditions and if you wear tights or jeans.

'Thrush', usually causing an itchy discharge, is especially common. If you suspect this use clotrimazole (Canesten) suppositories nightly for six nights or nystatin. An alternative is to take itraconazole 100mg oral tablets two in the morning and two in the evening for one day. This should not be taken if there is a possibility of pregnancy or if you are also taking antihistamines such as terfenadine (Triludan).

Trichomonas is a common cause of discharge, often offensive. The treatment is metronidazole 200mg tablets, two twice daily for seven days (again avoid if possibility of pregnancy and also avoid alcohol). See a doctor if your symptoms persist.

Sexually transmitted diseases (e.g. gonorrhoea or chlamydia) can cause a discharge and if you think there is a possibility of an STD try to see a reliable doctor. If this is not possible self-treat as under genital ulcer on page 193.

TAMPONS NOT AVAILABLE (or exorbitantly expensive)

Take plenty with you – enough for your whole assignment if supplies are not available at your destination. Check this out with an expatriate who has recently returned from the exact area and can give you reliable advice.

FAMILY PLANNING

If you are on the pill, take ample supplies of the preparation you are used to until you find out whether a reliable brand name of identical composition is available locally (see also pages 15–16).

For couples who have definitely decided not to have more children, it is worth giving serious thought to a permanent form of contraception (tubectomy or vasectomy) well before leaving, or early on in your next home leave. This reduces one form of stress which is at least largely under your control.

HEPATITIS

WHAT IS HEPATITIS?

Hepatitis is an infection of the liver caused by a virus, usually leading to jaundice in which the eyes and skin go yellow. Hepatitis A and B are preventable by immunisation and as far as travellers are concerned *should* be diseases of the past.

TYPES OF HEPATITIS

There are at least five different forms, but two are especially important.

Hepatitis A

This is the commonest form of jaundice in travellers, found almost world wide, most often picked up in the Indian sub-continent or tropical Africa. It is spread by the faeco-oral route – in other words germs from the faeces of an infected person contaminate the food and water drunk by another. It is therefore common wherever personal or public hygiene are poor. Those with hepatitis A nearly always make a complete recovery even though it may take time. The interval between becoming infected and developing your first symptoms (incubation period) is two to six weeks.

Hepatitis B

Also known as serum hepatitis, this is a less common but more serious form. It is spread in a similar way to AIDS, i.e. by having sex with a hepatitis B carrier, or through infected blood and dirty needles. However, especially in young children, it can also be caught by prolonged close contact with a carrier. Health workers are also at special risk. Hepatitis B occasionally leads to permanent liver damage and in the long term can cause liver cancer. The incubation period is six weeks to six months.

Other types of hepatitis

Together known as non-A non-B hepatitis, they include hepatitis C which is generally similar in symptoms and method of spread to hepatitis B, though more often comes from unidentified sources, and hepatitis E which resembles hepatitis A though it causes a serious illness in pregnancy.

SYMPTOMS OF HEPATITIS

All forms of hepatitis tend to start in a similar way – with headache, fever, chills and aching. Nausea or sickness usually occurs, often triggered by the smell of food or cigarette smoke.

There may be pain over the liver (the upper right side of the abdomen). The urine darkens and the eyes and skin usually become yellow.

At this stage it is common to feel very ill, exhausted and nauseated. After days or sometimes weeks the symptoms gradually improve, though full health may not be restored for up to six months.

Children and some adults may have a much milder illness, or even have hepatitis without knowing it. Those with hepatitis B are usually more seriously ill and symptoms persist for longer.

TREATMENT OF HEPATITIS

As with most viral illnesses there is no specific treatment. The key to recovery is *adequate rest*, usually in bed to begin with. Provided the body rests sufficiently it is usually able to fight off the illness. Those who fail to rest or return to work (or looking after their children) too quickly risk a longer illness or a relapse. Parents with young children will need maximum support and in some situations unaffected partners *will need to take time off work to look after the family*.

Plenty of sweet drinks, especially those containing glucose are claimed to ease the nausea. Intravenous glucose or fluids should be avoided unless vomiting makes it impossible to take fluids by mouth. There is no real evidence that special diets either help or hinder recovery.

Women who are on the pill are usually recommended to avoid it for about six months (and use alternative contraception!). It is also sensible to avoid alcohol until health has returned completely to normal.

Blood tests which monitor liver function (LFTs) can usually be arranged; though useful they are not essential except in severe illness. In some centres it is possible to confirm whether hepatitis A, B or C is the cause of the infection. Alternatively this can be done at a routine medical examination back home.

PREVENTION OF HEPATITIS

Hepatitis A and E are prevented by good personal hygiene, and following the advice on pages 35–48. Hepatitis B and C are prevented by following AIDS prevention advice.

Immunisations are of great value. All those aged 10 or over (or younger children at very high risk), unless known to have hepatitis A antibodies on a blood test, should have either a course of hepatitis A injections, or gammaglobulin every six months if going to a developing country (see pages 219–21).

All health workers serving in developing countries and all expatriates, especially children, residing or travelling for longer than six months should receive hepatitis B immunisation. If in doubt discuss this with your travel clinic or a specialist in travel medicine.

Patients with hepatitis A are at their most infectious before the jaundice develops, i.e. during the incubation period, and are thought to stop being infectious within two weeks after the jaundice starts. They can mix freely after the jaundice has faded. Those with hepatitis should use separate utensils and towels and take special care with personal hygiene. There is no need for strict isolation. Family contacts not known to have immunity or who have not received gammaglobulin in the past six months, or been immunised with Havrix, may gain some protection from gammaglobulin (but not Havrix) given as soon as a family member develops jaundice. This must come from a reliable (i.e. developed country) source.

Infection with hepatitis usually gives life-long immunity to that form of hepatitis.

Please see further details in Appendix F, pages 219–22.

INTESTINAL WORMS

Worms, or Helminths as they are known medically, are an occupational hazard of all but the most fastidious travellers and perhaps the commonest cause of a scream from the loo. Here are the most widespread:

PINWORMS (Threadworms, Enterobius)

You don't have to leave the UK to catch pinworms which are very common, especially amongst children. They are about 1cm long, whitish, and look like threads. They usually reveal their presence by being passed in the stool or by the *symptom* of anal itching especially at night. They are a nuisance but are not dangerous. *Prevention* depends on good personal hygiene. *Treatment* is with mebendazole 100mg (Vermox) one, twice daily for three days (not in children under twelve months or pregnancy) or piperazine (Pripsen), two doses separated by fourteen days.

ROUNDWORMS (Ascaris)

These are found throughout the tropics, especially affecting school-age children and those living amongst the local population. Roundworms look rather like earthworms; they are 20–30cm long, smooth, round and non-segmented.

Symptoms include abdominal pain, a distended abdomen or occasionally loss of weight. Often there are no symptoms and a junior member of the household discovers one or more, often with great astonishment, on passing a stool, or even worse during a vomiting attack. Eggs are often, *but not always*, found on stool tests. *Prevention* depends on careful food and personal hygiene. *Treatment* is with mebendazole 100mg, one, twice daily for three days.

HOOKWORMS (Ankylostoma)

Hookworms occur quite commonly in expatriates, especially those who go barefoot or wear unprotecting sandals or flip-flops. They are not noticed in the stool, but their eggs may show up on stool tests. Heavy infection with hookworm is harmful, especially in children because it leads to anaemia. Anyone who has *symptoms* of unexplained tiredness, shortness of breath or lack of energy should consider treating themselves for hookworm and having a haemoglobin test. *Prevention* depends on wearing shoes when walking outside the home. *Treatment* is with mebendazole one, twice daily for three days.

TAPEWORMS (Taenia)

You can become infected with tapeworm by eating under-cooked beef (T. saginata) or pork (T. solium). Tapeworms are long, flat segmented worms and sections may be noticed in the stool. Often they cause no obvious *symptoms* but their eggs, or worm segments, are found on stool tests.

Pork tapeworm occasionally leads to cysticercosis, a condition in which cysts can develop in other organs, causing for example, epileptic fits if one lodges in the brain. *Prevention* is through making sure that all meat, especially pork, is thoroughly cooked, meaning the centre of the meat should be brown or grey, not pink. *Treatment* is niclosamide 500mg tablets, four, chewed well, or praziquantel, under medical supervision.

A final suggestion

For expatriate families or anyone living amongst the local population in a developing country, there is much to be said for six-monthly treatment with mebendazole for all family members. The dose is one tablet (100mg) twice daily for three days for anyone over the age of 1 year (not recommended in pregnancy). This kills pinworms, hookworms, roundworms and whipworms, but not tapeworms.

LEISHMANIASIS

This disease comes in various forms – a serious illness affecting the whole body – visceral leishmaniasis (VL) or Kala Azar – rare in travellers but spreading in epidemic form in some areas of the world such as Sudan and north India. More important for the traveller is the skin form, cutaneous leishmaniasis (CL), more commonly known as oriental sore, and mucosal leishmaniasis (ML) which affects the mucous membranes of mouth and nose.

All forms of leishmaniasis are caused by a one-celled parasite known as Leishmania, passed on by the bite of a sandfly which is active at dusk and dawn. CL is found around the Mediterranean, parts of Asia and the northern half of Africa and causes an ulcerating nodule following a sandfly bite on an exposed part of the body, especially the face, legs and arms. It may develop days, months or even years after the bite and though not serious can leave a disfiguring scar.

ML is found in tropical America and gives a severe, ulcerating sore around the mouth and nose (Espundia), again leaving permanent scarring.

To *prevent* leishmaniasis avoid sandfly bites in affected areas. Use insect repellents and permethrin-impregnated bed nets, or sleep on the roof. Report to a doctor any bite which persists or ulcerates.

MENINGITIS

Meningitis is an infectious illness which causes inflammation of the brain lining. There are several forms, many caused by viruses spread by contaminated food and water. They commonly cause abdominal upsets and severe headache which settle without treatment.

A much more serious form is caused by an organism known as Meningococcus, or Neisseria, and the rest of this section refers to this form of the disease. It is spread by breathing in the germs from infected people or from healthy carriers. Meningococcal meningitis is found in many tropical countries, including the Sahel (countries bordering the southern Sahara, known as the 'Meningitis belt'), though epidemics occur in countries to the south and the north of this area. There have been recent outbreaks in many parts of Africa and it is also found in the Indian subcontinent, and parts of South America and Mongolia.

The disease comes in various strains, and vaccines have been developed against forms A and C which are common in Africa and S. Asia, but not yet against form B, responsible for South American cases. Meningitis tends to occur in the cool season when people crowd together – in the Sahel this coincides with our winter.

Symptoms include fever, severe headache, neck stiffness, nausea or vomiting, often preceded by a blotchy rash. Often meningitis is known to be present in the area. Children are at special risk.

The illness caused by forms A and C can be prevented by a single immunisation (see Appendix F). Those visiting areas where the disease is known to occur, especially if working with children or in crowded communities, should consider immunisation, as should all children visiting affected areas. Anyone who has had their spleen removed should be immunised for any overseas travel. During epidemics it is wise to avoid crowded conditions.

Treatment needs to be started immediately by a doctor, as the disease can cause death within hours. In an emergency, health workers can give penicillin G two mega units, one injection intramuscularly into each buttock.

Please see further details in Appendix F, pages 223–4.

MIGRAINE AND HEADACHES

Migraine and headaches in general often become worse when working overseas. Stress, dehydration and missing meals can contribute to this. Sudden changes of altitude can also make headaches worse.

If you have a tendency to migraine, discuss in detail with your doctor before you travel how you will manage this. Take plenty of your preferred medication with you. A good first-line *treatment* is one tablet of metoclopramide 10mg (Maxolon: prescription needed in UK), or domperidone (Motilium – not in pregnancy), followed ten minutes later by either soluble aspirin total 900mg (usually three tablets) or soluble paracetamol total 1,000mg (usually two tablets). Keep your fluid intake up and consider a sweet snack between meals. Some find that giving up tea, coffee, chocolate or alcohol helps, though it may take you at least two weeks to become de-addicted, during which time headaches may be worse. Migraine can be worsened by the contraceptive pill.

It is worth knowing that there is a range of treatments available for migraine both for prevention and cure and if the medication you have been using is not working it is worth trying another. Most GPs are experienced at dealing with migraine.

If headaches still seem to be getting worse review your lifestyle and see if there are any changes you can make to reduce stress and overwork. Look at ways in which you can relax both on the job or at home or how you might get away for a break or a holiday.

If headaches worsen for no obvious reason, or persist, or start for the first time this may be caused by a wide variety of infections and other conditions, including malaria. It would be sensible to consult a doctor.

PLAGUE

Plague, well known as the cause of the Black Death, still causes occasional outbreaks in parts of Asia, Africa and South America. Zaire, India, Madagascar and Mongolia have recently reported cases. Although the risk to travellers and expatriates is extremely remote, the fear of plague can cause much anxiety and it is therefore worth knowing about its prevention.

Plague is *caused* by a bacterium which affects rodents (especially rats), and occasionally other mammals including humans. It is spread by fleas which come from an infected (often dying) animal looking for another host. A bite from an infected flea causes *bubonic* plague, but a person so infected may pass on the germs through coughing or breathing to others who then develop *pneumonic* plague.

Symptoms develop within a week and in the case of bubonic plague include severe shivering, high temperature and pain, and swelling in the groin or armpit, caused by inflamed glands (bubos). Untreated cases have a 50/50 chance of survival.

Pneumonic plague starts and progresses rapidly with fever, cough and severe shortness of breath, death usually occurring within forty-eight hours.

Prevention of plague consists of avoiding areas where outbreaks are known to be *currently* occurring. If this is not possible take every effort to avoid flea bites by applying insect repellent and sleeping on permethrin-impregnated sheets or bed nets. Both bed nets and sheets must be well tucked in as fleas can otherwise jump from the floor to the bed. Bed legs should ideally be stood in jars of water. Kill off any potentially infected rodents, especially rats in or near the house. Regularly treat domestic pets with flea powder. Plague vaccines are not currently recommended, except for vets and zoologists working in affected areas.

Consider taking preventative antibiotics in the following three situations: definite contact with a case of plague; being in crowded areas where pneumonic cases are occurring; and the possibility of a flea bite from an infected animal.

Adults and children over the age of 8 should take tetracycline or oxytetracycline 250mg tablets four times daily for one week, if necessary repeating this if further contact occurs. Children between the ages of 2 and 8 if at high risk can take ciprofloxacin 10mg per kg daily in two divided doses for one week. (Ciprofloxacin is not otherwise used in children.) Children under the age of 2 and pregnant women should avoid areas where plague cases are occurring.

Treatment, if you develop any suspicious symptoms, must start immediately and be under medical supervision. The same antibiotics are used – twice the above dose of tetracycline or oxytetracycline, and 15mg per kg of ciprofloxacin.

RABIES

NOTE: Even if you have had a course of three rabies injections before going abroad, you will still need further injections if you are bitten, licked or scratched by an animal which may have rabies (see below).

WHAT IS RABIES?

Rabies is a virus infection of man and other mammals, caused by a bite, lick or scratch from an infected mammal. Certain mammals are well known as 'reservoirs' of infection. Examples are the dog almost worldwide, the fox in Europe, and vampire bats in South America and the Caribbean. However any mammal may be infected, and can in turn pass on the infection.

Rabies is found in over 150 countries, though the following are free: the United Kingdom, Australia and New Zealand, Norway and Sweden, Japan, Papua New Guinea and most Pacific Islands. Rabies is especially common in the Indian sub-continent, Afghanistan, Thailand including Bangkok, Vietnam and the Philippines, and parts of tropical Latin America and Africa.

RISK TO TRAVELLERS

As a traveller or expatriate you have two risks which both need preventing: the small but important one of being infected with rabies, and the more common experience of anxiety following an encounter with a suspicious animal which you did nothing about. By being well informed and appropriately vaccinated you can be well protected against both these risks. Your maximum risk times are when travelling in rural areas, trekking, or jogging, or where touching an apparently friendly but unknown dog.

THE SYMPTOMS OF RABIES

These are well known. In animals there is often a change of behaviour, a dog being more aggressive or more docile than usual. There may be an aversion to water. Unprovoked attacks by dogs or by any animal which behaves aggressively should raise alarm bells, especially if rabies is common in the area. *Some infected (and infectious) animals behave quite normally.*

Humans can develop symptoms any time from four days to two years after being bitten (usually thirty to sixty days).

The symptoms progress rapidly from fever and headache to paralysis, bouts of terror and aggression to coma and death. There is no cure once symptoms have started.

PERSONAL PROTECTION FROM RABIES

This is through a series of three injections with Human Diploid Cell Vaccine (HDCV) or equivalent before travelling abroad. More details are given in the section on Rabies Vaccine, in Appendix F. HDCV is a simple, and safe vaccine, given into the upper arm, with minimal side-effects. All those spending six months or more in an area where rabies exists should have this as should those on shorter journeys if travelling off the beaten path or in areas where rabies is known to be present. Remember however that these injections will *not* necessarily give you full protection.

When first taking up residence in a developing country identify a safe source of HDCV (and HRIG – see below) by asking your embassy or another reliable source of information.

Keep antirabies injections up-to-date on domestic pets, especially dogs (see page 47).

ACTION AFTER BEING BITTEN, LICKED OR SCRATCHED BY A SUSPICIOUS ANIMAL

• Wash the wound carefully with soap and water, if possible under a running tap to remove infected saliva and dirt. Apply either tincture of iodine or alcohol (gin or whisky will do). It is better not to scrub. The wound should not generally be sutured.

• Consider any animal as potentially rabid which is *either* behaving strangely, *or* is unknown, *or* which disappears. Try to identify and observe the animal for ten days. Any animal alive after this time can be considered safe.

• Start rabies injections as follows using one of the regimes below:

Either:

The short regime – if you have definitely had a course of three primary injections in the past, with subsequent boosters every two to three years.

You should now have: 1 dose of 1ml HDCV at the time of the bite and another 3–7 days later by the intramuscular route into the deltoid muscle (upper arm).

Or:
The full regime – if you have *not* had a full course of preventative injections with regular boosters as recommended above.

You should now have: 1ml of HDCV on days 0, 3, 7, 14, 30, 90, by the intramuscular route, the exact timing of the latter two not being critical.

In addition you will need to have an injection of either Human Rabies Immune Globulin (HRIG) 20 units per kg body weight OR Equine Antirabies Serum (EARS) 40 units per kg body weight. HRIG and EARS should be given *after* HDCV: both may be hard to obtain. In either case half is infiltrated around the bite and half given by IM injection. Because EARS may cause an allergic reaction a doctor should be present with a supply of adrenalin, and ideally a skin test should be done first.

If the animal is alive after ten days rabies injections can be discontinued.

● In many developing countries post-mortem tests on the brain of an infected animal cannot be relied upon. However where good facilities exist a brain fluorescent antibody test can be arranged.

● Ensure that your tetanus cover is up-to-date, and also that any infection is treated promptly with antibiotics.

SPECIAL SITUATIONS

Delays

If *either* there is a delay in starting HDCV of more than forty-eight hours, *or* if HRIG or EARS have been given *before* HDCV, *or* the person at risk is either elderly, malnourished or with lowered immunity, the first HDCV should be trebled and given at three different sites of the body.

Even with longer delays of days or weeks it is still worth starting a course of HDCV injections if you come to recognise that you have had a suspicious encounter.

Rabies and children

Children and toddlers with their love for furry beasts have a higher risk of being exposed to rabies. Actively discourage them from touching unknown animals. Preventative injections are only recommended from the age of 1 year upwards but post-exposure treatment is given regardless of age.

Rabies and pregnancy

Pregnant women are not normally given prophylactic injections, but post-exposure treatment is essential and no serious reactions have been reported.

• If a local doctor suggests that a single injection or tablets alone are sufficient, *do not accept his advice*.

For further details on rabies immunisation, see Appendix F, pages 225–6.

RIVER BLINDNESS (Onchocerciasis)

This is found in scattered areas of tropical Africa, and less commonly parts of Central America and the Yemen. It is spread by black flies (2–4mm long), appropriately known as Simulium damnosum. They usually breed near fast-flowing rivers. Untreated the illness can eventually lead to blindness, rare in travellers unless repeatedly reinfected. Those working in rural areas where the disease is known to occur are at risk.

Symptoms include an initial bite, often painful, which may be followed by skin nodules, especially over the lower trunk. Often itching or an itchy rash is the first symptom and this, along with swollen lymph nodes, may develop many months, or up to three years, after leaving the affected area. Eye symptoms are rare in travellers.

Prevention includes covering the skin and using insect repellents. Those working in high-risk areas can take prophylactic treatment under specialist advice. *Treatment* with ivermectin is effective but should be under medical supervision. Long-term follow-up is needed.

If you have been working in an area where oncho is known to occur you should have a blood test on return. You should also report any symptoms described above even if they start many months after leaving the tropics. A skin snip test at a Tropical Disease Unit usually confirms the diagnosis.

SEXUALLY TRANSMITTED DISEASES

These are theoretically the easiest diseases to *prevent*. You can forget about them if either you practise abstinence or have sex only in the context of a long-term stable relationship with a partner known to be unaffected. Pre- or extramarital sexual encounters always carry with them the risk of picking up a sexually transmitted disease, especially if you don't use a condom. Even in those committed to a risk-free lifestyle it is easy to slip up during a time of stress, loneliness – or celebration.

Those diseases which are always, or most frequently transmitted sexually include: syphilis, gonorrhoea, chlamydia, lymphogranuloma, chancroid, trichomonas, genital herpes, pubic lice, hepatitis B and HIV infection.

There are two *symptoms* which should alert you to the probability of an STD – genital ulcers and a penile discharge. Vaginal discharge and pelvic pain have a greater variety of causes (see page 178).

If you suspect you may have an STD try to see a reliable doctor as soon as possible. If this really is not feasible you can self-treat as follows:

Penile discharge or genital ulcers: Tetracycline 500mg four times daily or doxycycline 100mg twice daily for seven days, or ciprofloxacin 500mg single dose. These drugs are not suitable in pregnancy – instead use erythromycin 500mg four times daily for fifteen days.

Vaginal discharge: for treatment of this common condition see page 178.

On return home it is important to have a full medical check and also to consider having an HIV test along with an opportunity for counselling and discussion.

SKIN CONDITIONS

The combination of sun, heat, biting insects and lack of hygiene means that skin problems are common in developing countries. Aid workers, adventure travellers, children, and volunteers on low budgets need to take special care.

BLISTERS

These can develop very quickly, may be slow to heal and often become infected.

Prevent them by wearing well-fitting shoes, loose cotton socks and if trekking or walking any distance, by *wearing-in your shoes or boots for several days before*. Sandals, especially if worn without socks in dusty areas, quickly lead to blisters.

Treat blisters as follows: if the skin is broken, wash carefully, apply antiseptic cream and a non-adherent bandage, secured with an adhesive dressing. If unbroken leave intact if possible, otherwise pierce roof of blister with sterile needle, apply gauze covered with thin layer of Vaseline and secure with adhesive dressing. Avoid offending footwear.

BOILS AND INFECTED BITES

These are very common in the tropics, often developing at times of overwork, stress or when due for home leave or a holiday. They often start as bites which become infected through scratching.

Prevent boils by trying to develop a balanced lifestyle with adequate rest and relaxation; eat a well-balanced diet with fresh fruit and vegetables. Wash regularly with soap and water. Salt water is helpful either through bathing in the sea (where unpolluted) or, if you are prone to boils, by adding salt to bath water where possible. If living in an institution make sure your sheets are properly cleaned, and take care over your laundry.

Treat boils as follows: wash gently with soap and water and apply antiseptic cream. Do not squeeze, especially if on the head or neck, but allow the boil to come to a point and burst naturally, at which time you can apply absorbent gauze with vaseline. Larger boils, especially in the armpit, may need lancing by a doctor or nurse using a sterile blade.

Those with a tendency for troublesome boils should take flucloxacillin caps 500mg every six hours for a week, or if allergic to penicillin, cotrimoxazole (Septrin, Bactrim) two tablets twice daily for one week or erythromycin 500mg every six hours for one week, in each case starting when the boil first develops. Also apply an antiseptic cream, e.g. Naseptin, up both nostrils twice daily for a week, ideally in all household members – especially children – as the bacteria causing boils are carried in the nose. If you are troubled by boils take a supply of one of these antibiotics and Naseptin with you (see also page 109 for prevention of flea bites).

Boils are occasionally caused by tumbu flies (see page 111).

CREEPING ERUPTION (Larva migrans)

This is caused by a larva which penetrates the skin and causes a red, slowly moving itchy line. It is usually caught on tropical beaches where dogs are common.

The chief *symptom* is a red itchy line, usually either on the sole of the foot or the buttock. It can be *prevented* by lying on a towel rather than directly on the beach, and by walking barefoot only *below* the high tide mark. It can be *treated* either by allowing it to disappear naturally, or by taking albendazole 400mg tablets, two daily for five days.

FUNGUS INFECTIONS (Tinea)

Fungi like warm, moist conditions and are therefore very common in tropical climates. The main *symptom* is a red, rough itchy patch, often circular with a spreading edge.

Athlete's foot (Tinea pedis) causes itching between the toes; groin itch (Dhobie's itch, Tinea cruris) causes itching in the groin and between the legs. Other 'ringworm' infections occur in the scalp or anywhere on the body surface.

Thrush commonly causes a reddish line in the folds of the groin and the breast, especially in the overweight: thrush is also the commonest cause of itchy vaginal discharge (see page 178). You can help to *prevent* fungus infections by bathing regularly, wearing loose-fitting cotton underpants (Dhobie's itch), and open-toed shoes or sandals with cotton socks changed daily (athlete's foot). Trainers or any shoe with an internal rubber sole are more likely to lead to athlete's foot.

You can *treat* it by applying an antifungal dusting powder, e.g. Mycota, between the toes and into the socks (athlete's foot) and for other fungus infections by applying clotrimazole cream (Canesten), three times daily until two weeks after symptoms have cleared. Fungal infections (except thrush) which fail to clear, respond to griseofulvin tabs 500mg twice daily until at least all signs of the infection have disappeared, or to itraconazole 100mg one daily for fifteen days (see Appendix A). Avoid both of these in pregnancy.

Travellers often notice a scaly rash with some paling of the skin, usually over the back and trunk. This is known as Pityriasis versicolor and is best treated by an antifungal cream such as terbinafine applied for two weeks.

PRICKLY HEAT

This is an itchy condition, common in children and those not acclimatised, caused by the blocking up of sweat ducts. *Symptoms* consist of small reddish spots on a pinkish skin, which develop mainly on the upper trunk, armpits, waist and the backs of the knees and neck. It disturbs sleep and can be very irritating, especially for children.

You can *prevent* it by wearing light-fitting cotton clothing, and by avoiding excessive soap. Dust talcum powder into clothes that rub against the skin.

It is best *treated* by applying calamine lotion and keeping as cool as possible. Air conditioning helps to reduce it, but most expatriates improve anyway after acclimatisation.

SKIN CANCER

Those most at risk from skin cancer include long-term residents of the tropics, the fair-skinned and anyone exposed to prolonged or excessive sun in childhood. Make sure you take sensible precautions to avoid too much sun (see pages 102–4).

The two commonest cancers are:

Malignant melanomas: these usually arise in existing moles. If a mole starts to enlarge, darken, become less regular, or begins to itch, ooze or bleed report it to a doctor.

Basal cell carcinomas (BCCs or rodent ulcers): these are locally malignant but do not spread to other parts of the body, meaning treatment is always successful. The face is the commonest site, and they usually occur in older people. If you notice any persistent nodule, lump or rough patch which ulcerates, oozes or bleeds see a doctor. It could be a BCC or another form of skin cancer which needs more urgent treatment.

In addition older people or those exposed to years of sun often develop scaly, sometimes darkened patches on the face, neck, forearms or backs of the hands. If you have these, known as solar keratoses, show them to a doctor as occasionally they lead to skin cancer. Equally, if you have lived in a hot climate for a long time or are worried about your skin, have this looked at during your regular tropical check-up on return home.

See also page 24 to see how pre-existing skin conditions are likely to be affected by tropical conditions.

SLEEPING SICKNESS (Trypanosomiasis)

Sleeping sickness is present in scattered rural areas across tropical Africa, and in some areas is becoming commoner. It is caused by the bite of an infected Tsetse fly (about 1cm in length, and like a large housefly), which flies during the day (see diagram). Expatriates visiting known areas, especially on wildlife safaris in east Africa or working on development programmes, are at slight risk of getting it.

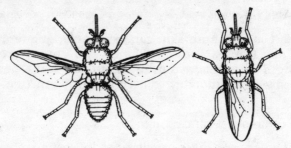

Tsetse fly (about 1cm long)

Symptoms start with a boil-like, usually painful, swelling at the site of the bite. Fever may then develop within two to three weeks (east Africa), sometimes months later (west and central Africa), often with enlarged lymph nodes, especially in the neck. Headache and drowsiness gradually increase.

If you have suspicious symptoms consult a doctor experienced in tropical diseases without delay. *Treatment* must be under medical supervision, but *prevention* is quite straightforward: use insect repellents, cover exposed areas of your body and avoid wearing the colour blue (a favourite with many Tsetses) when in known areas.

TICK BITE FEVER (Tick-borne relapsing fever)

Tick bite fever is found mainly in east Africa, e.g. Tanzania, but cases also occur in west Africa and elsewhere in the tropics. It is caused by an organism known as Borrelia which is spread by infected ticks which live in cracks and crevices, and bite during the night. Those sleeping in mud huts in known areas are at risk.

Symptoms depend on the area. Commonly TBRF mimics malaria with high fever, head and muscle ache and vomiting, with symptoms usually lasting four to seven days. It commonly relapses after about seven further days, sometimes on repeated occasions, each attack gradually becoming less severe. It is dangerous in pregnancy.

Treatment is with tetracycline tablets 250mg four times a day for one week. (An alternative should be used in pregnancy.) However symptoms should first be treated as for malaria unless this has been excluded on a blood slide.

Prevention is to avoid sleeping in mud huts in areas where the disease is known to occur, using insect repellents and mosquito nets, sleeping as high off the floor as possible and removing any ticks as soon as they are discovered (see page 110).

TONSILLITIS AND SORE THROATS

You will not necessarily escape such mundane problems as colds and sore throats by living in the tropics. If you have suffered from tonsillitis before going abroad you may well find this recurs, especially at times of stress, overwork or exhaustion.

The *symptoms* of tonsillitis are fever, sore throat and swollen lymph nodes. Very occasionally throat infections may be caused by diphtheria (foul breath, greenish membrane on throat).

Prevention is to give priority to holidays, one day off in seven, and trying to achieve a balanced lifestyle. If you have a tendency to tonsillitis, consider starting antibiotic treatment *as soon as symptoms start*.

If you have had several severe attacks in the recent past discuss with your doctor whether you should have a tonsillectomy.

Many sore throats and most attacks of tonsillitis are caused by a germ called Streptococcus (Strep throat) and any sore throat, especially if accompanied by swollen neck glands and a fever, is worth *treating* with antibiotics for ten days.

Use either penicillin V 250mg four times daily or amoxycillin 500mg three times daily. If you are allergic to penicillin try erythromycin 500mg four times daily or cotrimoxazole two, twice daily. Some people find that gargling with aspirin can soothe the pain, but this should not be used in those under 12. Remember however that many sore throats are caused by viruses and although antibiotics will cause no harm, neither will they make any difference.

Glandular fever is a common cause of sore throat, especially in younger travellers (see page 170).

TOOTH PROBLEMS

REASONS FOR TAKING TOOTHCARE SERIOUSLY

Severe toothache and dental abscesses are surprisingly common in those living overseas. It is worth giving your teeth a high degree of priority for the following reasons:

• Severe toothache can ruin a visit, an important programme or a holiday.

• Tooth abscesses often occur when you are tired or run-down as for example during a tough assignment or at the end of a volunteer year.

• Dental care overseas is often unreliable, may be very expensive and carries a small but definite hepatitis B and HIV risk in some countries.

• The water used as a coolant or to rinse your mouth may be contaminated.

RECOMMENDATIONS FOR LOOKING AFTER YOUR TEETH

• Have a thorough dental check well before you leave. Have any fillings attended to, any ill-fitting dentures replaced and any pre-emptive treatment of impacted or painful wisdom teeth. Whenever you come on leave have a further check.

• Choose any dentist overseas with care and on personal recommendation. Check as far as you are able that all needles and syringes are sealed, disposable and not reused; also that all instruments are steam-sterilised.

• Consider taking an emergency dental kit and a supply of antibiotics (see p. 202 and Appendix A).

COMMON DENTAL PROBLEMS

• *Toothache*. This may be caused either because of injury, the loosening of a filling or because a dental abscess is starting to form. If pain becomes severe or prolonged try to find a reliable dentist and start treatment with antibiotics in the meantime, as detailed below. Oil of cloves can ease the pain, as can aspirin placed at the base of the tooth.

• *Tooth abscess*. This is usually obvious because of severe pain on moving the tooth or pressing the root. Sometimes you may develop a swollen cheek or jaw (which may be painful or painless). *Treat* an abscess by taking antibiotics such as amoxycillin 500mg three times a day for seven days (not if allergic to penicillin) or cotrimoxazole (Septrin, Bactrim) two, twice daily for seven days (but not in pregnancy), and see a dentist, who may either remove the tooth or recommend root canal treatment. If the latter enquire *carefully* how many treatments are likely and the cost of each.

• *Lost dentures*. Consider taking a spare pair and try to remove them before an attack of vomiting.

• *An avulsed front tooth*. If clean, soak in salty boiled water and replace within half an hour, pressing in firmly the right way round, and getting to the dentist as soon as possible.

• Known heart problems such as past history of rheumatic fever, heart valve disease, or presence of prosthetic valves. Antibiotic cover will be needed for all dental work – discuss this with your dentist before going overseas. Widely used is amoxycillin 2gm by mouth thirty minutes before and 1gm six hours after any dental work, or if allergic to penicillin erythromycin 1.5gm before and 1gm after.

PREVENTING TOOTH PROBLEMS

This is through regular dental cleaning, at least twice a day. Dental floss is valuable. Avoid excessive sweets and too much oversweetened tea or soft drinks, unless there is nothing else safe to drink.

A small amount of fluoride helps prevent tooth decay, too much leads to tooth mottling and discolouration. Natural levels of fluoride in the water tend to be higher in tropical countries. Use fluoride tablets only if local levels are known to be very low or absent. Fluoride tooth paste can still be used but make sure children don't eat it.

A DENTAL KIT

These are available and widely used by those living in remote conditions or where dental facilities are unreliable. They usually contain equipment for temporary replacements of crowns, bridges and caps as well as material for temporary fillings. After using a kit see a reliable dentist as soon as you can. If you take a kit, make sure you also have a supply of antibiotics.

TUBERCULOSIS

Expatriates occasionally develop TB, usually if they have been working with TB cases, or living long-term amongst the local population. With the spread of AIDS, TB is becoming commoner, meaning that those working in HIV-affected areas are at an increased risk.

Tuberculosis is most commonly a disease of the lungs, caused by infection spread from an infectious case or from reactivation of a previous (often unknown) lesion. Only rarely is it spread in the tropics from infected milk. TB is common in most tropical areas especially the Indian subcontinent and sub-Saharan Africa.

Symptoms include loss of weight, fever and declining health, plus symptoms specific to the organs involved. Most commonly the lungs are affected giving persistent cough with sputum, sometimes bloodstained, chest pain and evening fever. Children may simply lose weight or fail to gain it, only developing specific symptoms later.

TB is partly *prevented* by having a BCG vaccination. This is only given if a tuberculin test (Mantoux, Heaf or Tine test) carried out before is negative, showing that no natural immunity is present. Babies and young children who have not knowingly been exposed to TB can be given BCG without prior testing (see Appendix F, page 217).

Everyone going to live for any length of time in a developing country should make sure they have either had a BCG vaccination or a positive tuberculin test. As immunity may not be lifelong, adults at high risk should not depend on the BCG they had at school but should be retested and given BCG if negative, unless a scar from a previous BCG is present. Similarly those serving long-term overseas in high-risk occupations should consider retesting at ten-yearly intervals to ensure their immunity is still sufficient. It is worth noting that American guidelines on the use of BCG differ widely from British.

If you develop suspicious symptoms either abroad or after you come home consult a doctor as soon as possible. You should have a special TB microscopy and culture of any sputum you cough up as well as a chest X-ray and repeat tuberculin test. If TB is caught early it can be fully *treated* using multi-drug therapy under careful medical supervision.

URINARY TRACT INFECTION (UTI)

The *symptoms* of this are usually obvious – an urge to pass urine, accompanied by pain or a burning sensation. Hot, bumpy journeys, dehydration and increased sexual activity on holidays can contribute. For expatriates living in hot climates, urinary infections are sometimes associated with a kidney or bladder stone.

Women tend to get urinary infections more commonly than men, and any infection in a man should always be investigated by a doctor, as should repeated infections in a woman. Children who start, or restart, wetting their bed for no obvious reason may have a urinary infection.

If you are unable to see a doctor or arrange a urine test *self-treat* with either trimethoprim 100mg, 2 tablets twice daily for 5 to 7 days, or cotrimoxazole (Septrin, Bactrim) two, twice daily for 5 to 7 days, not in pregnancy. If there is a risk of having a sexually transmitted disease, greatly increase your fluid intake and treat as for genital ulcer on page 193.

It is sensible to have a urine test on return home to make sure no infection persists. A medical check as soon as possible is essential if there is any possibility of a sexually transmitted disease.

YELLOW FEVER

Yellow fever is a virus infection found in the tropical belt of South America, and in Africa, especially Nigeria. It is unknown in Asia. Although there have been more cases of YF reported between 1985 and 1990 than any other five-year period since 1948, the risk to travellers is small, and becomes negligible in those immunised within the past ten years.

Yellow fever is spread by the bite of an Aedes mosquito. 'Jungle' yellow fever is found in forested areas and is spread by mosquitoes from infected monkeys. 'Urban' yellow fever is spread by the mosquito from an infected person. In practice those at greatest risk are forest workers in Brazil and children in west Africa.

Symptoms comprise fever, abdominal pain, vomiting and headache, followed by signs of kidney and liver failure including jaundice. Symptoms always develop within six days of being infected. There is no specific *treatment*, but *prevention* is easy – a reliable, safe vaccine repeated every ten years (see Appendix F).

APPENDIX A

CHECKLIST OF USEFUL MEDICINES

A supply of medicines or a medical kit is worth taking with you if you are working in a remote area or a place where you cannot easily obtain or trust essential medicines.

Prepacked kits are available (see Appendix C for suppliers). Alternatively you can make up your own.

Please consult manufacturer's instructions and the text in this manual for further details, notes of side-effects, interactions with other drugs, safety in pregnancy and when breastfeeding, and for exact dosages.

Dosages given are those commonly used for adults. They refer to the drugs listed in capitals, *not* to the alternatives.

Items marked # are available on prescription only. They can be obtained from your doctor, usually on a private rather than on an NHS prescription. Drugs not so marked are available over the counter.

Generic (scientific) names are given first; common brand names are in brackets.

P = avoid in pregnancy; B = avoid if breastfeeding.

BASIC LIST

This is a suggested list of standard items for a tropical health kit (common alternatives are given).

Name	How used	Disease	P or B
ANTACID tablets (various brand names)	One or two as needed	Indigestion, heartburn	
# CHLORAMPHENICOL eye ointment	Apply three or four times daily	Eye infections	
CHLORPHENIRAMINE 4mg tabs (Piriton) or terfenadine (Triludan)	One, four-hourly as needed	Allergy, hay fever, itching	
CLOTRIMAZOLE cream (Canesten) or miconazole (Daktarin)	Rub in as needed	Fungal infections	
# COTRIMOXAZOLE 80/400mg tabs (Septrin, Bactrim) or co-amoxiclav (Augmentin) (penicillin-based) or amoxycillin (penicillin-based)	Two, twice daily for one week	General purpose antibiotic for those able to take sulfa drugs	P
DEET-containing repellent (Autan, Jungle Formula)	Rub in as needed	Insect repellent	
HYOSCINE tabs (Kwells) or cinnarizine (Stugeron)	One as needed	Travel sickness	

Drug	Dosage	Use	
LOPERAMIDE 2mg tabs (Imodium) or diphenoxylate (Lomotil)	Two, then one, four-hourly	Emergency treatment of diarrhoea	
# MEBENDAZOLE 100mg tabs (Vermox)	One, twice daily for three days	Treatment of pin, round, whip and hookworm. (Not in children under 1)	P
# METOCLOPRAMIDE 10mg tabs (Maxolon)	One, three times daily as needed	Nausea, sickness	P
# METRONIDAZOLE 400mg tabs (Flagyl, Zadstat) or tinidazole (Fasigyn)	Two, three times daily for five days	Amoebiasis, giardiasis	P
ORAL REHYDRATION SALTS (Dioralyte, Rehidrat)	One sachet with water, frequently	Diarrhoea, dehydration	
PARACETAMOL 500mg tabs (Panadol) or aspirin tabs	Two, four- to six-hourly	Pain, fever	
SAVLON antiseptic cream	Rub in as needed	Infected skin	

208   *Good Health, Good Travel*
SUBSIDIARY LIST

You should also consider whether you need any of the following:

	For prevention/treatment		
ANTIMALARIALS		See text	
CALAMINE lotion	Apply as needed	Sore, inflamed, itchy skin	
# CIPROFLOXACIN 250mg tabs (Ciproxin)	See text	Prevention/treatment of diarrhoea, treatment of typhoid – not usually in children or adolescents	P, B
# CLOTRIMAZOLE suppositories (Canesten) or nystatin	Insert one for six nights	Vaginal thrush	P, B
# DOXYCYCLINE 100mg tabs (Vibramycin)	See text	Prevention of diarrhoea. Treatment of cholera. Not in children under 8–12	P, B
HYDROCORTISONE cream	Rub in as needed	Eczema, reaction to insect bites	
# ITRACONAZOLE 100mg tabs	Vaginal thrush: two twice daily for one day. Fungal skin infections: one daily for fifteen days	Avoid if taking antihistamines	P, B
OIL OF CLOVES	Apply to painful tooth and gum	Toothache	
SENNA tabs (Senokot)	Two at night, as needed	Constipation	
# TEMAZEPAM 10mg tabs (Normison)	One as needed	Difficulty in sleeping	

APPENDIX B

CHECKLIST OF FIRST AID KITS

Please see pages 10–14 for further details of the types of kit recommended. A wide variety of kits is available from suppliers (see Appendix C) to cover the varying needs of travellers. Alternatively you can make up your own.

A simple first aid kit could contain some or all of the following:

Crepe bandage
Plasters/band aids
Micropore tape
Triangular bandage
Cotton wool
Skin closure strips
Mediswabs
Non-adherent dressings
Rubber gloves
Gauze swabs
Scissors
Safety pins
Tweezers
Savlon liquid, e.g. as Savlodil sachet
Clinical thermometer (preferably non-mercury)

You may also wish to take a needle and syringe kit in case of needing sterile supplies in an emergency. This could include some or all of the following:

Needles – small, medium, large
Syringes – 2ml and 5ml
Malaria lancets
Mediswabs
Skin suture with needle
Skin closure strips
Non-stick dressings
Surgical tape

If in addition you plan to travel extensively in areas where HIV disease is common you may wish to take an AIDS Protection Kit which in addition to the above would include an intravenous giving set and blood substitute.

APPENDIX C

LIST OF SUPPLIERS

InterHealth, 157 Waterloo Road, London SE1 8US (0171 928 8681): and phone needed:

Provide a wide range of low-cost health kits, antimalarial equipment, medicines and books specifically designed for travellers, volunteers and those working abroad. Also run a travel and immunisation clinic.

Echo, 2 Ullswater Crescent, Coulsdon, Surrey CR3 2HR (0181–660 2220, fax: 0181–668 0751):

Provide a wide range of bulk-supply medicines and equipment for overseas health projects.

Mission Supplies Ltd, Alpha Place, Garth Road, Morden, Surrey SM4 4LX (0181–337 0161, fax: 0181–337 7220):

Provide a range of both small and large equipment needed by both people and programmes overseas.

Masta Ltd, 51 Gower Street, London WC1E 6HJ (0171–631 4408, fax: 0171–323 4547):

Provide a sterile medical equipment pack, and other supplies.

Nomad, 3–4 Wellington Terrace, Turnpike Lane, London N8 0PX (0181–889 7014, fax: 0181–889 9529):

Provide clothing, equipment, kits, also run a pharmacy and immunisation clinic.

APPENDIX D

LIST OF TRAVEL HEALTH FACILITIES

1. TRAVEL CLINICS

Travel clinics provide a full range of immunisations, health advice for those going abroad and usually a variety of useful equipment and books. There is a large network of British Airways Travel Clinics throughout much of the UK. Phone 0171–831 5333 to find out the address of the one nearest to you. Remember too that GPs can arrange most immunisations, many of them on the NHS.

Travel clinics in London include:

● InterHealth, 157 Waterloo Road, London SE1 8US. Tel: 0171 928 8681.

● Trailfinders Ltd, 194 Kensington High Street, London W8 7RG. Tel: 0171-938 3999; fax: 0171–938 3305.

● Nomad, 3–4 Wellington Terrace, Turnpike Lane, London N8 OPX. Tel: 0181–889 7014; fax: 0181-889 9529.

2. DEPARTMENTS OF TROPICAL MEDICINE

You can be seen at any of the following if you are referred by your GP or 'off-the-street', if you are suffering from a tropical emergency such as malaria:

● Hospital for Tropical Diseases, 4 St Pancras Way, London NW1 OPE. Tel: 0171–387 4411.

● Liverpool School of Tropical Medicine, Pembroke Place, Liverpool L3 5QA. Tel: 0151–708 9393.

● Department of Communicable and Tropical Diseases, Birmingham Heartland Hospital, 45 Bordsley Green East, Bordsley Green, Birmingham B9 5SS. Tel: 0121–766 6611.

● Infectious Diseases Unit (& Travel Clinic) Ward 17, City Hospital, Greenbank Drive, Edinburgh EH10 5SB. Tel: 0131–536 6000, ext: 66122.

● Communicable Diseases Unit, Ruchill Hospital, Glasgow G20 9NB. Tel: 0141–946 7120.

Your first point of contact should normally be your GP. Alternatively you can attend the accident and emergency department at your nearest district general hospital if you have a serious or sudden health problem on return from overseas.

3. HEALTH CARE FOR EXPATRIATES SERVING ABROAD

InterHealth provides comprehensive health care including medicals, psychiatric support and counselling, for any expatriate or volunteer serving abroad with a mission, aid agency or non-governmental organisation. Contact Dr Ted Lankester or Miss Jackie Hall at InterHealth, Partnership House, details on p. 210.

Care for Mission provides a similar range of services for members of Christian missions and aid agencies. Contact Dr Michael Jones, Care for Mission, Ellem Lodge, Duns, Berwickshire TD11 3SG, Scotland. Tel: 01361 890677 Fax: 01361 890329.

4. SOURCES OF SPECIALIST ADVICE

AIDS

The national AIDS helpline is 0800 567123.

The UK NGO AIDS Consortium provides advice on funding and technical assistance for projects, and a book *The Guide for Overseas Employers*. Contact Sue Lucas, UK NGO AIDS Consortium. Tel: 0171–401 8231.

Alcohol

The National Alcohol Helpline is 0345 320202.

Back pain

The Back Pain Association can be contacted on 0181–977 5474.

Blood donation

The National Blood Transfusion Service will tell you how and where to give blood (and find out your blood group). Tel: 0345 711711.

Careers and job vacancies

The Christian Service Agency matches jobs with personnel available for the Christian sector. Contact CSA, Holloway Street West, Lower Gornall, Dudley, W. Midlands DY3 2DZ.

REACH have lists of vacancies in part-time charitable work for retired professionals. Tel: 0171–928 0452.

InterChange specialises in careers advice for those returning from overseas. Contact Joy Lankester on 01892 661421.

Counselling

InterHealth can arrange counselling for anyone who has been working overseas with a charitable organisation.

The British Association for Counselling can be contacted on 01788 550899.

Diabetes

The British Diabetic Association has useful information on travel. Tel: 0171–323 1531.

Disability

Two organisations provide helpful information:

The Disabled Living Foundation. Tel: 0171–289 6111.

RADAR. Tel: 0171–637 5400.

Foreign Office Advice Line

Worldwide details on safety for travellers. Tel: 0171–270 4129 and 4179.

Health Line

The Hospital for Tropical Diseases has an automated recorded phone advisory service on 0839 337722/33.

Insurance

Banner Financial Services specialise in travel and health insurance for members of voluntary agencies. Tel: 01342 717917; fax: 01342 712534.

Malaria

There are pre-recorded messages on antimalarials and also advice in case of special difficulty on 0891 600350.

Marriage enrichment

Mission to Marriage runs courses countrywide from a Christian perspective. Tel: 01638 713047.

Relate (previously the Marriage Guidance Council) have trained counsellors throughout the United Kingdom. Contact them at local centres.

Medical Advisory Service for Travellers Abroad

MASTA provide detailed briefs on immunisations, recommended antimalarials and health hazards for each country of the world. Tel: 0891 224100.

Medic Alert

Provide bracelets, tags etc. for those with allergies or special conditions. Tel: 0171-833 3043.

Rape and personal safety

The Susie Lamplugh Trust provides details on the awareness and avoidance of situations involving personal danger. Tel: 0181–392 1839.

Sunburn

The Sunburn Helpline is 0800 556655.

Travel agents

Key Travel specialise in economic fares for members of charitable organisations: 92–96 Eversholt Street, London NW1 1BP. Tel: 0171–387 4933. Fax: 0171–387 1090.

Trailfinders arrange low-cost prices worldwide for any traveller. Tel: 0171–938 3999. Fax: 0171–938 3305.

5. OVERSEAS TROPICAL HEALTH DEPARTMENTS

Australia

Commonwealth Institute of Health A27, University of Sydney, NSW 2006. Tel: 660 9292. Further information on departments of travel and tropical medicine from the secretary, Commonwealth Department of Health, PO Box 100, Woden, ACT 2606.

Belgium

Institut de Medecine Tropicale Prince Leopold, Nationalestraat 155, 2000 Antwerp.

Canada

Missionary Health Institute, 4000 Leslie Street, Willowdale, Ontario M2K 2R9.

Tropical Medicine Department, Toronto General Hospital, Toronto, Ontario M5G 1L7. Tel: 416 595 367.

France

Hopital de la Pitie-Salpetriere, Blvd de l'Hopital, 75013 Paris.

Holland

Royal Tropical Institute (Kononlijk Institut voor de Tropen), 63 Mauritskade 1092 AD, Amsterdam, Holland.

Ireland

Tropical Medical Centre, 5 Northumberland Avenue, Dun Laoghaire, Co. Dublin, 010–3531–280–4996. Contact Dr Graham Fry.

New Zealand

Infectious Diseases Unit, Auckland Hospital.

Russian Federation

American Medical Centre, in Moscow and St Petersburg, contact AMC on 0101–7095–956–3366 or 256 (8212) (USA) for further details.

USA

There are many specialist travel and tropical health departments. Contact the Centre for Disease Control (CDC), Atlanta, Georgia. Tel: 0101 404 639 3311 for further information.

Details of appropriate health care facilities in developing countries can be obtained from MASTA – for a fee (address above).

APPENDIX E

INCUBATION PERIODS OF IMPORTANT ILLNESSES

The incubation period is the time between being infected by an organism (e.g. from the bite of a mosquito, the swallowing of a diarrhoea-causing organism) until the first symptoms appear. This can be useful as it may help you to work out what disease may be causing (or not causing) your symptoms.

Amoebiasis	At least 7 days, sometimes weeks or months.
Bilharzia (schistosomiasis)	4 weeks or more.
Brucellosis	1 month or more.
Chicken pox	2–3 weeks.
Cholera	A few hours to 5 days.
Dengue fever	5–8 days.
Diphtheria	1–5 days.
Filariasis	6 months or more.
Food poisoning (bacterial)	Variable: 1 hour to 12 days.
German measles (rubella)	2–3 weeks.
Giardiasis	Usually 2–6 weeks.
Gonorrhoea	2–7 days.
Hepatitis A	2–6 weeks.
Hepatitis B	6 weeks–6 months.
Herpes (genital)	2–12 days.
HIV infection	2 weeks to 10 years or more.
Jap. encephalitis	4–14 days.
Lassa fever	3–21 days.
Leprosy	Usually 2–4 years; occasionally shorter or much longer.
Malaria	Usually about 2 weeks. May be much longer: is never less than 8 days.
Measles	1–2 weeks.
Meningococcal meningitis	Usually 1–3 days. Always less than 1 week.
Mumps	2–3 weeks.
Onchocerciasis (River blindness)	1 year or more.
Plague	Usually less than 1 week.
Polio	10–15 days.
Rabies	2 weeks to more than 1 year.
Scabies	2–6 weeks.
Sleeping sickness	2 weeks–2 months.
Syphilis	10 days to 10 weeks.
Tetanus	Usually about 2 weeks; may be much quicker or much longer.
Tick bite fever	3–11 days.
Typhoid	Usually about 10 days. Can vary between 3 and 60.
Typhus	4–14 days.
Visceral leishmaniasis	3 months or more.
Yellow fever	3–6 days.

APPENDIX F

NOTES ON INDIVIDUAL VACCINES

BCG (FOR TUBERCULOSIS)

TYPE OF VACCINE: live, injected intradermally. BCG gives partial protection only.

A Tuberculin test (also known as a Mantoux, Heaf or Tine test) is often given before BCG to see whether immunity is present. Positive means there is immunity, and that BCG is not necessary.

COUNTRIES WHERE TB IS A RISK: all developing countries, especially Asia, tropical Africa and South America. TB is on the increase in most areas of the world.

RISK TO TRAVELLERS: those with no immunity are at risk especially if working or living in close contact with the local population.

NUMBER AND SPACING OF DOSES: there are three categories for those travelling to at-risk situations.

• Babies and young children should be given BCG.

• Older children and adults who have never had BCG should be tested to see whether they have immunity. If they test negative they should be given BCG.

• Adults at higher risk who were tested more than ten years ago (and where negative received BCG), can be retested and given BCG, if now negative, unless a scar is present from a previous immunisation. This retesting is only necessary for health workers or those who will be in very close contact with TB patients.

BCG gives a significant degree of protection after two months. It is not known exactly how long this protection lasts.

PRECAUTIONS: BCG should not be given to anyone seriously ill or with high fever. It is not safe in pregnancy.

HOW OBTAINED: some GPs, and most travel clinics can arrange testing and give BCG: others will refer you to a clinic where this can be done. Adults wishing to be retested or to arrange repeat BCG often encounter difficulties.

REACTION WITH OTHER VACCINES: can be given at the same time

as other killed or live vaccines. If not given on the same day as other live vaccines, three or more weeks should be left between them. For those requiring gammaglobulin this should ideally be given at least three weeks after BCG (or three months before).

CERTIFICATION: none necessary.

RECOMMENDATIONS: all those travelling to a developing country should either have had a positive Tuberculin test or have received BCG. Those at higher risk (see above) should ideally be retested every ten years (unless a previous scar is present) and be given a repeat BCG if negative. See also under dose and spacing above. American guidelines differ.

CHOLERA VACCINE

NOTE: The World Health Organisation does not routinely recommend the use of this vaccine as it is only 50–60% effective, lasts only a short time and does not prevent the spread of cholera. It is given mainly so that a genuine certificate can be shown to the few countries who still (against WHO recommendations) ask to see one, or if visiting severely affected areas.

A new live cholera vaccine may soon be available which is likely to be more effective and will give longer immunity.

TYPE OF VACCINE: killed, injectable.

COUNTRIES WHERE CHOLERA OCCURS: cholera is present year round in much of tropical Africa, southern Asia, and parts of Latin America. Cholera now affects more countries and greater numbers of people than for many years.

RISK TO TRAVELLERS: generally very low provided you observe good standards of hygiene, and avoid contaminated water and food. These hygiene precautions are more important than the vaccine.

NUMBER AND SPACING OF DOSES: for certification a single dose is sufficient. This is valid for six months starting six days after vaccination. The full course is two injections separated by at least one week and preferably one month, with booster doses every six months.

First dose gives (partial) protection after six days, subsequent boosters give immediate (partial) protection.

PRECAUTIONS: cholera vaccine should not be given to anyone with fever, known hypersensitivity, in pregnancy, or to children under twelve months. Side-effects include local soreness and redness, and commonly headache and fever in the first forty-eight hours.

HOW OBTAINED: cholera is usually available free under the NHS from general practitioners, but doctors may charge for the certificate.

REACTION with other vaccines: none. May be given at the same time but at a different site.

CERTIFICATION: this is still asked for by some countries. Check with your travel health adviser a few weeks before your date of departure.

RECOMMENDATIONS: cholera vaccine should be given only if the country you are visiting is known to ask for a certificate, or to front-line workers or travellers in epidemic situations.

HEPATITIS A VACCINE (Havrix Monodose and Havrix Junior)

NOTE: this highly effective vaccine has largely superseded the use of gammaglobulin for trips abroad longer than three months, and for frequent travellers.

TYPE OF VACCINE: killed, injectable.

COUNTRIES WHERE HEPATITIS A OCCURS: worldwide, but especially common in developing countries.

RISK TO TRAVELLERS: adults and older children are at risk. Those under about 10 years of age, when infected with hepatitis A, usually have a less severe or unrecognised illness and then develop lifelong immunity.

NUMBER AND SPACING OF DOSES: one 1ml dose of Havrix Monodose provides coverage for up to one year. A booster dose six to twelve months after the first gives persistent immunity for up to ten years. It is given by intramuscular injection into the deltoid muscle. Children under 16 should be given the Havrix Junior 0.5ml, two to four weeks apart, and a booster dose six to twelve months later.

Protection takes effect between two and four weeks after the first dose.

PRECAUTIONS: should not be given to anyone seriously ill, with high fever, or known hypersensitivity to the vaccine. Side-effects are usually mild, with slight soreness and redness at the injection site, and less often fever, headache and nausea. Pregnant women should receive gammaglobulin rather than hepatitis A vaccine.

REACTIONS WITH OTHER VACCINES: none. May be given at the same time but at a different site.

HOW OBTAINED: is usually available on the NHS to those travelling to developing countries. Can also be given at travel clinics. Some doctors will want to check your hepatitis A antibodies before giving it, or use gammaglobulin for trips of three months or less.

STORAGE: should be kept between 2° and 8°C, and should be protected from light. Should not be frozen. Is thought to retain its potency if briefly warmed in transit for up to about seven days. Has a short shelf-life of two years.

RECOMMENDATIONS: hepatitis A Monodose is recommended for those aged 16 and over travelling to developing countries for three months or more or who are regular travellers. If travelling for more than twelve months an additional booster should be given (see above). Pregnant women, and unimmunised contacts of infectious cases are currently recommended to receive gammaglobulin instead. Anyone who has lived in a developing country for two years or more, has had a history of jaundice or IV drug abuse, or was born before about 1942 should first have a hepatitis A antibody test and only be immunised if this is negative; others can be tested at the doctor's discretion.

CHILDREN aged 10–16 should receive Havrix Junior. Those under 10 are not usually immunised unless going to very high-risk areas.

NB (1): anyone immunised with original as opposed to Monodose Havrix should receive their booster with original, not Monodose. Monodose has been used in the UK since May 1994.

NB (2): A new formulation of Havrix Junior with single dose is likely to be released in 1995.

GAMMAGLOBULIN – AGAINST HEPATITIS A

NOTES:

1. Gammaglobulin gives *valuable protection* against hepatitis A for at least three months.

2. Gammaglobulin, known to have been recently manufactured in the UK, western Europe, North America, Australia and New Zealand, is safe and free from any AIDS risk. Supplies manufactured in developing countries *should never be used*.

TYPE OF VACCINE: a protein (immunoglobulin) derived from human serum. It gives passive, short-lived but valuable protection.

COUNTRIES WHERE HEPATITIS A OCCURS: worldwide, but especially common in developing countries.

RISK TO TRAVELLERS: adults and older children are at risk. Those under about 10 years of age, when infected with hepatitis A, usually have a less severe or unrecognised illness and then develop lifelong immunity.

NUMBER AND SPACING OF DOSES: a dose according to manufacturer's instructions, ideally within one to two weeks of departure. Gives protection immediately.

PRECAUTIONS: can be safely given to anyone unless a known hypersensitivity exists. Side-effects amount to no more than sore buttocks for twenty-four hours. Serious reactions are rare. Can be given in pregnancy

HOW OBTAINED: usually free on the NHS for those travelling to developing countries.

REACTIONS with other vaccines: none with any killed vaccines or with yellow fever vaccine which can be given at the same time though at a different site. Gammaglobulin may reduce the effectiveness of the following live vaccines: oral polio, mumps, measles, rubella and BCG, oral typhoid, oral cholera. It should ideally be given at least three weeks after (or three months before) these vaccines, though there is no danger from the injection if these intervals are not followed.

RECOMMENDATIONS: recommended for pregnant women travelling to developing countries. Short-term travellers (three months or less) can have either gammaglobulin or hepatitis A vaccine. Those known to have hepatitis A antibodies (see above) do not need to be immunised with either gammaglobulin or hepatitis A vaccine. Non-immune contacts of infectious cases should be given gammaglobulin rather than hepatitis A vaccine.

HEPATITIS B VACCINE

NOTE: because hepatitis B is a serious illness and can lead to liver cancer later in life, the World Health Organisation is drawing up plans to introduce universal immunisation.

TYPE OF VACCINE: killed, injectable.

COUNTRIES WHERE HEPATITIS B IS A RISK: worldwide, but most common in Africa, southern and SE Asia, China, the Pacific Islands and parts of South America.

RISK TO TRAVELLERS: generally (though not exclusively) spread in a similar way to AIDS, therefore blood transfusions, dirty needles and sexual intercourse with carriers are the main methods of spread. Health workers have an increased risk, as do very young children who can catch it through close contact with a carrier.

NUMBER AND SPACING OF DOSES: there are two methods:

Regular course: three injections, leaving at least one month between the first and second, five months between the second and third (0, 1, 6), given by intramuscular route.

Quick course if insufficient time for regular course: three injections at intervals of at least one month followed by a booster one year after the first (0, 1, 2, 12).

Whichever course you have followed, boosters can be given every three years. Where full cover is important, e.g. amongst health workers, a blood test can be done to see whether a booster is necessary, or it can be carried out two to four weeks after completing a course or having a booster to ensure a sufficient level of antibody has developed. (100 iu/ml or more).

The vaccine gives protection immediately after the third dose, or after any booster. It can be given at any age.

PRECAUTIONS: hepatitis B vaccine should not be given to anyone with fever, or known hypersensitivity either to the vaccine or to yeast. It should be avoided in pregnancy (unless risk very high). Side-effects include local soreness, occasionally with nodule formation, and fever, nausea and headache.

HOW OBTAINED: the vaccine is available from travel clinics and on the NHS to doctors, nurses, dentists and some paramedics. Occasionally GPs will also give these free to anyone planning to live or work in a developing country.

STORAGE: if you need to take doses abroad with you the vaccine should be kept between 2° and 8°C. It is thought to remain effective if temporarily heated up to 25°C for between four and six days, provided it is then rerefrigerated. It should not be frozen.

REACTION with other vaccines: none. May be given at the same time but at a different site.

RECOMMENDATIONS: all health workers, or those working with drug abusers or the mentally handicapped, should be protected regardless of their length of stay. Others, particularly children, living or working in developing countries for more than six months should consider protection. Further advice can be obtained from your travel health adviser.

JAPANESE ENCEPHALITIS VACCINE

TYPE OF VACCINE: killed, injectable.

COUNTRIES WHERE THE DISEASE OCCURS: SE Asia, parts of India (especially Nepal border area and the south), Nepal, China, Japan, Korea, Pakistan (especially Sind).

RISK TO TRAVELLERS: low except in known high-risk districts during and shortly after the rainy season, where those residing in rural areas especially where pigs are kept, are at some risk.

NUMBER AND SPACING OF DOSES: two injections, at an interval of seven to fourteen days with a booster after one year and then every three years. Protection takes effect fourteen days after the second dose and shortly after any booster dose. A different regime (e.g. in USA) is sometimes recommended of three injections at 0, 7 and 30 days. Children aged 1 to 3 should receive half the dose and those under twelve months should not be given the vaccine.

PRECAUTIONS: the vaccine should not be given to anyone who has had a serious reaction to a previous dose, nor to anyone with a fever, cancer or with any serious illness especially of the heart, liver, or lung. It should not be given in pregnancy. Side-effects include local soreness, occasional fever and headache. More serious reactions have occasionally been reported after second or subsequent doses, sometimes hours or days after the injection.

HOW OBTAINED: expensive and not available on the NHS. It is available from travel clinics and some GPs will order it and give it privately.

REACTION with other vaccines: none. Can be given at the same time but at a different site.

RECOMMENDATIONS: only recommended for travellers spending one month or more during the time of year, and at a location where the disease is known to occur. Consult your travel health adviser if in doubt.

MENINGITIS VACCINE

NOTE: this vaccine protects only against meningococcal meningitis strains A and C, two of several serious forms of meningitis.

TYPE OF VACCINE: killed, injectable.

COUNTRIES WHERE THIS STRAIN OF MENINGITIS OCCURS: 'the Meningitis Belt' – countries bordering the southern Sahara (the Sahel) are permanently affected. From time to time the disease spreads southwards, northwards and westwards, usually during the dry season, to affect other African countries. Meningitis A and C also occur in other parts of the world notably the Indian subcontinent and Mongolia.

RISK TO TRAVELLERS: an appreciable risk occurs during outbreaks or when visiting the meningitis belt during the dry season. Children, or those working with children are at greater risk.

NUMBER AND SPACING OF DOSES: a single dose of 0.5ml at least three weeks before departure, with boosters every three years. Form 'AC Vax' can be given from two months of age, form 'Mengivac' from eighteen months. Gives protection after fifteen days.

PRECAUTIONS: should not be given to anyone with fever or severe illness, known hypersensitivity nor during pregnancy unless risk very high. Side-effects include local soreness, and occasional chills and fever in the first twenty-four hours.

HOW OBTAINED: not normally free under the NHS though many GPs will obtain it or write a prescription for you to collect. Otherwise it is available in travel clinics.

REACTIONS with other vaccines: none. Can be given at the same time but at a different site.

RECOMMENDATIONS: as described above. Also needed (with certificate) for all going on Haj pilgrimage to Saudi. Those who have had their spleen removed must have this vaccine, regardless of country of travel. The distribution of meningitis changes frequently. Consult your travel health adviser a few weeks before departure.

POLIO VACCINE (ORAL:OPV:SABIN)

TYPE OF VACCINE: live, oral. In some countries, killed, injectable polio vaccine is used instead (IPV:SALK).

COUNTRIES WHERE POLIO OCCURS: most developing countries, especially the Indian subcontinent. No new case of paralytic polio has been confirmed in South America since 1991.

RISK TO TRAVELLERS: generally low except where outbreaks occur. Although polio is becoming less common in many areas because of immunisation programmes, all travellers should still be protected.

NUMBER AND SPACING OF DOSES: most children and those born after 1956 (when the vaccine was introduced) should have received a primary course of three injections. For such people boosters are needed every ten years to guarantee immunity.

Those who have not had a primary course of three in the past, or who are unsure, should do so before going abroad, with three injections at intervals of one month or more.

PRECAUTIONS: should not be given to anyone with fever, serious illness, diarrhoea and vomiting, or those with low immunity. It should not be given in pregnancy. There are usually no side-effects.

HOW OBTAINED: polio vaccine is generally free on the NHS, though adults requiring a primary course may be charged.

REACTIONS with other vaccines: may be given on the same day as any other vaccine, live or killed. In the case of other live vaccines, if not given on the same day should be given at an interval of three weeks or more. Those needing gammaglobulin should ideally receive this three weeks or more after (or three months before) polio vaccine.

RECOMMENDATIONS: all travellers should be in date for polio. Expatriate children brought up overseas must be fully immunised.

RABIES VACCINE (HDCV)

NOTE: contrary to the fears of some, modern rabies vaccine is both simple and safe. It *does not however* give full protection and after any encounter with a potentially rabid animal further doses are needed.

TYPE OF VACCINE: killed injectable 'Human Diploid Cell Vaccine' or HDCV.

COUNTRIES AFFECTED BY RABIES: present in almost 150 countries, i.e. virtually worldwide EXCEPT the UK, Norway, Sweden, Australia, New Zealand, Japan, Singapore, Papua New Guinea and most Pacific islands. High risk areas include the Indian subcontinent, SE Asia, especially Thailand and the Philippines, China and parts of Africa and South America.

RISK TO TRAVELLERS: the risk to most careful travellers is relatively low, but intrepid travellers, rural workers, vets, zoologists and children are at higher risk. Many travellers and expatriates worry that their last encounter with a suspicious dog might have sealed their fate.

NUMBER AND SPACING OF DOSES: three injections are needed with seven to fourteen days between the first and second, about twenty-one between the second and third (0, 7–14, 28). Boosters are needed every two to three years, or every year for those working with animals. If longer than three years has elapsed since your last booster the full course must be repeated. An alternative regime of two intradermal injections twenty-eight days apart gives almost as good protection and is sometimes used.

Gives protection after second or third dose, BUT two further injections are still needed after a bite or lick from a suspect animal, the first ideally immediately after the bite and the second between the third and seventh day (0, 3–7). If preventative rabies injections have not been completed or have lapsed, six post-exposure injections are needed along with Human Rabies Immunoglobulin (HRIG). See page 189.

Rabies injection should usually be given by the intramuscular (IM) route (into the upper arm, not the buttock). Nurses very experienced with the technique can give the injection intradermally using only one tenth of the IM dose. Injections given to those who are currently taking chloroquine should generally include the full dose via the IM route, as chloroquine may reduce the effect of the intradermal injection.

The vaccine is thought to retain its potency for a cumulative total of fourteen days if unrefrigerated. It should however be kept as cool as possible, ideally being placed in a Thermos. It must not be transported in the aircraft hold where freezing may destroy it.

Rabies injections in children under the age of twelve months may not be fully effective (though they are sometimes used from six months onwards). For this reason you should take enough rabies vaccine with you so that children can be immunised from the age of 1 year upwards.

Rabies vaccines are increasingly becoming available in developing countries. Purified Chick Embryo Culture Vaccine (PCEC) is considered to be safe and effective provided it has been kept reliably refrigerated since manufacture (hard to verify). It is used in the same way as HDCV. Purified Vero Rabies Vaccine (PVRV) and Purified Duck Embryo Vaccine (PDEV) are also acceptable.

PRECAUTIONS: rabies vaccine should be avoided in anyone with a high fever or seriously ill. Pregnant women should only receive it if their risk is very high, though after any possible exposure it is essential. Side-effects are few and include local swelling and redness and occasionally fever and headache.

HOW OBTAINED: not usually available on the NHS but some GPs, at their discretion, are prepared to provide rabies injections at low cost to those who are going to live or travel in areas where the disease is found. It is available from travel clinics.

REACTIONS WITH OTHER VACCINES: none. Can be given at the same time but at a different site.

Advantages of having rabies injections before going abroad:

• It reduces the number of further HDCV or equivalent injections you need after an encounter with a suspicious animal, from six to two.

• It means you will not need a special immunoglobulin (HRIG or EARS) injection as well.

• It limits the risk of delays in obtaining vaccine when in remote areas, allowing you forty-eight hours before having post-exposure injections.

RECOMMENDATIONS: those going to affected areas whose occupation, style of travel or remoteness puts them at risk, or who may be more than twenty-four hours from a reliable source of vaccine, should be immunised, regardless of their length of stay; so also should all those, including children over twelve months of age, spending six months or more in a country where rabies is known to occur.

TETANUS TOXOID (TT) or combined with low dose diphtheria (Td/Dip Tet bis)

TYPE OF VACCINE: killed, injectable.

COUNTRIES WHERE TETANUS OCCURS: worldwide but much commoner in the tropics, rare at high altitudes.

RISK TO TRAVELLERS: in the absence of completed immunisation any wound, even a trivial one, may cause tetanus. So also may delivery, surgery, middle ear infections, bites and boils.

NUMBER AND SPACING OF DOSES: those born after 1961 will normally have received a course of DPT in childhood and those who have served in the armed forces a course of TT. Others should make sure they have completed a primary course of three injections before travelling abroad. The best spacing is six to eight weeks between the first and second, four to six months between the second and third, but three injections at monthly intervals will confer full immunity. Travellers may find difficulty obtaining a booster after any injury or accident abroad, and are therefore recommended to have boosters every five years, rather than the normally recommended ten years, in order to maintain full protection.

Protection takes effect immediately after the third dose or any booster.

PRECAUTIONS: should not be given to anyone with high fever or seriously ill, or with known hypersensitivity. May cause fever and pain at the injection site especially if less than five years have elapsed since last booster. It is safe in pregnancy.

HOW OBTAINED: Tetanus Toxoid, DPT and Td are usually available on the NHS.

REACTIONS WITH OTHER VACCINES: none. Can be given at the same time but at a different site.

RECOMMENDATIONS: all those travelling overseas should have completed a primary course of three Td, TT or DPT injections at some time in their lives and have had a booster within the past five years. It is now best practice to use Td vaccine rather than TT (when available).

TYPHOID VACCINE (TYPHIM Vi)

TYPE OF VACCINE: killed, injectable.

COUNTRIES WHERE TYPHOID OCCURS: the Indian subcontinent, Indonesia and other parts of Asia, tropical South America and Africa.

RISK TO TRAVELLERS: there is an appreciable risk.

NUMBER AND SPACING OF DOSES: a single injection gives substantial protection for three years. Boosters are needed every three years. Protection takes effect fourteen to twenty-one days after the injection.

PRECAUTIONS: should not be given to anyone with a fever, or seriously ill, nor to those under eighteen months. It should only be given in pregnancy if the risk is high. Side-effects include minor pain, swelling and redness at the injection site for two to three days with occasional mild fever or headache. Side-effects are less marked than with the traditional whole cell vaccine.

HOW OBTAINED: available under the NHS and from travel clinics.

CERTIFICATION: not normally required.

REACTION WITH OTHER VACCINES: none. May be given at the same time but at a different site.

RECOMMENDATIONS: travellers to developing countries from 5 years upwards should be immunised. Children between eighteen months and 5 years and pregnant women should only be covered if the risk of catching the disease is high. Precautions with food and water are essential.
Note: the traditional whole cell vaccine (typhoid monovalent) is still used though side-effects are more troublesome. TAB is now obsolete. Live oral typhoid vaccine (Vivotif) is used in some centres as an alternative to Typhim Vi, but three doses are necessary, and it has to be taken according to very detailed instructions.

YELLOW FEVER VACCINE

TYPE OF VACCINE: live, injectable.

COUNTRIES WHERE YELLOW FEVER OCCURS: tropical Africa between approx 16° north and 16° south: tropical South America between approx 10° north, and 20° south.

Some countries within this belt are reportedly free.

RISK TO TRAVELLERS: there is an appreciable risk in several countries in the YF zone, especially to rural travellers.

NUMBER AND SPACING OF DOSES: a single injection to all those over nine months of age, with a booster every ten years.

PRECAUTIONS: should not be given to anyone with fever, who is seriously ill, has depressed immunity, is allergic to neomycin, polymixin or hens' eggs. YF vaccine should not be given to children under nine months, nor to pregnant women unless travelling in a high risk area. Side-effects which involve about one person in ten include local pain, headache and fever five to ten days after the injection.

HOW OBTAINED: from Yellow Fever Vaccination Centres. Your travel health adviser or GP will advise you where the nearest one is. It is not available under the NHS.

REACTIONS with other vaccines: can be given at the same time as any other vaccine but at a different site. Being a live vaccine, if not given on the same day as other live vaccines, it should be given at an interval of three weeks or more. There is no interaction with gammaglobulin which can be given at the same time, or any time before or after YF.

CERTIFICATION: an international certificate should be filled in and carried when travelling abroad. It is valid for ten years, taking effect ten days after the first vaccination and immediately after any further dose. Some countries outside the YF zone will demand to see a valid certificate if you have travelled from or passed through a country within the zone in the last six days. An exemption certificate should be carried by anyone who for any reason cannot be vaccinated.

RECOMMENDATIONS: Anyone nine months or over travelling through or residing in a country in the YF zone should keep their injection and certificate up-to-date.

FURTHER READING

Except where otherwise indicated, the following may be obtained from bookshops

ON LIVING ABROAD:

The Tropical Traveller, J. Hatt, 3rd edition 1993, Penguin. A highly informative and amusing read.

The Daily Telegraph Guide to Working Abroad, G. Golzen Kogan Page, 14th edition 1991.

ON HEALTH CARE WHILE ABROAD:

Traveller's Health, Dr Richard Dawood, Oxford University Press (475 pages). Regular new editions. A standard reference book for the serious traveller.

Where There is No Doctor, D. Werner MacMillan, 1993, and special Africa Edition. A really valuable book for anyone living in areas with absent or unreliable health services. Available from bookshops, InterHealth etc.

Health Advice for Travellers, Department of Health, 1994 and updated annually. Basic information directed at tourists and concentrating on Europe. Free from post offices or tel: 0800 555777.

International Travel Health Guide, S. D. Rose, 1994 and updated annually. Travel Medicine Inc., USA. A comprehensive book written from the American viewpoint.

Travel in Health, G. Fry, V. Kenny, 1994, International Safari Health, Dublin. An easy-to-read book for tourists and travellers. Tel: 0101-3531-280-4996 to order a copy.

Health Literature Hotline (0800 555777). Details of government publications on health and travel.

International Travel and Health – vaccination requirements and health advice, WHO, Geneva, 1994 and updated annually. Available from WHO Distribution and Sales, 1211 Geneva, along with details of wide range of books on health.

Healthy Travel: Bugs, Bites and Bowels, J. W. Howarth. Cadogan, 1995.

First Aid Manual, authorised manual of St John/St Andrew Ambulance, British Red Cross, Dorling Kindersley, 1993.

FOR EXPEDITIONS AND ADVENTURE TRAVEL

Expedition Medicine, ed. B. Juel-Jensen. Expedition Advisory Centre, 5th edition, 1994. This and other helpful books on expeditions are available from EAC, Royal Geographical Society, 1 Kensington Gore, London SW7 2AR.

FOR THE DISABLED AND ELDERLY

Travel and Health in the Elderly: A Medical Handbook, I. B. McIntosh, Quay Publishing, 1992.

Guide for the Disabled Traveller, Automobile Association, 1991. Available from the AA.

Nothing Ventured: Disabled People Travel the World, A. Walsh (ed.), Rough Guide Series (Penguin), 1991.

FOR THOSE WITH CHILDREN

In the Tropics with Children, F. G. Fry et al, Royal Tropical Institute, Amsterdam, 1989. A handy and useful guidebook. Available from Kononlijk Institut Voor de Tropen, 63 Mauritskade, 1092 AD Amsterdam, Netherlands.

FOR THOSE IN STRESSFUL SITUATIONS

Honourably Wounded, M. Foyle, Marc Europe, 1987. Very useful insights and suggestions, written specifically for those involved in Christian work overseas, all of whom should obtain a copy before leaving.

EVALUATION SHEET

We hope you have found this manual useful. In order to make improvements in the next edition please take time to complete this evaluation sheet and send it to Dr Ted Lankester, InterHealth, UK, 157 Waterloo Rd, London SE1 8US.

DETAILS ABOUT YOURSELF

Please indicate the overall length of time you are likely to spend or have spent in the country of your assignment.
□ Under 6 weeks □ 6 weeks to 3 months □ 4 months to 6 months
□ 7 months to one year □ 1–2 years □ 3–5 years □ More than 5 years

Please indicate the term which describes you most accurately.
□ Volunteer □ Christian missionary □ Christian aid worker
□ Aid worker □ Student □ Short-term visitor □ Adventure Traveller
□ Tourist □ Businessman/woman □ Journalist □ Diplomat
□ Member of armed forces

Please indicate your age.
□ Under 15 □ 15–20 □ 21–30 □ 31–40 □ 41–50 □ 51–60 □ Over 60

Please indicate your sex.
□ Male □ Female

Please indicate which describes you best:
□ Child (under 18)
□ Single
□ Married with no children
□ Married with young children (average age below 18)
□ Married with grown up children (average age 18 or above)
□ Separated/divorced
□ Widow/widower

Now please complete the following, in each case circling the most accurate description.

COVERAGE
Did you find the SCOPE (ie number) of subjects covered:
□ Too great □ About right □ Too restricted

Did you find the average DEPTH of coverage of articles:
□ Too detailed □ About right □ Not detailed enough

Please list any five subjects covered you found most helpful/relevant.

_____

_____

Please mention any subject covered you did not find helpful/relevant.

_____

_____

Were there any subjects not included which you feel should be added to a subsequent edition?

_____

_____

ACCURACY
Did you notice any technical or editorial mistakes?

_____

_____

STYLE
Did you find the style:
□ Too heavy □ About right □ Too light

Do you have any other suggestions about style?

_____

_____

LAYOUT
Please suggest any ways in which the layout could be improved.

_____

_____

ILLUSTRATIONS
Do you have any comments about the number, style and scope of illustrations?

_____

_____

PRICE
In terms of value for money did you feel the price of the book was
□ Too high □ About right □ Too little

GENERAL
What did you feel were the best features of the book?

What did you feel were the least good features of the book?

Do you have any other suggestions about how to improve the book?

Thank you for taking the time to complete this form.

INDEX

Italic numerals indicate main references